Divinely Enough

Embracing the Woman God has Called You to Be

MELISSA HARTS

WestBow
PRESS
A DIVISION OF THOMAS NELSON

WestBow Press books may be ordered through booksellers or by contacting:

WestBow Press
A Division of Thomas Nelson
1663 Liberty Drive
Bloomington, IN 47403
www.westbowpress.com
1-(866) 928-1240

Scriptures taken from the Holy Bible, New International Version®, NIV®. Copyright ©
1973, 1978, 1984, 2011 by Biblica, Inc.™ Used by permission of Zondervan. All rights
reserved worldwide. www.zondervan.com The "NIV" and "New International Version" are
trademarks registered in the United States Patent and Trademark Office by Biblica, Inc.™
All rights reserved.

All Scripture quotations in this publications are from The Message.
Copyright (c) by Eugene H. Peterson 1993, 1994, 1995, 1996, 2000,
2001, 2002. Used by permission of NavPress Publishing Group.

ISBN: 978-1-4908-0199-5 (sc)
ISBN: 978-1-4908-0201-5 (hc)
ISBN: 978-1-4908-0200-8 (e)

Library of Congress Control Number: 2013912645

Printed in the United States of America.

WestBow Press rev. date: 9/3/2013

Dedicated to my blessing and inspiration, Katieri, and to all the young women who need to hear that they are divinely enough just as they are.

CONTENTS

INTRODUCTION

A woman in harmony with her spirit is like a river flowing.
She goes without pretense and arrives at her destination,
prepared to be herself and only herself.

—Maya Angelou

I am forty-four years old, and I have spent too much of my life working on being *just* enough. I leave it to erudite psychologists and sociologists to determine if the reason for that is societal, hereditary, or simply due to my own baggage, but wherever it comes from, it has been with me for too long. On any given day throughout my life, I may awaken to the gnawing feeling that I am not smart enough, pretty enough, thin enough, light-skinned enough, motherly enough, wifely enough ... okay, you get the picture. I have lived with these feelings of not measuring up and have accepted them as a natural appendage of my very being. But my feelings of inadequacy and not belonging slapped me in the face the morning I had an innocent conversation with my daughter in our kitchen. She was only eight years old; yet her words revealed a truth that I had buried deep within myself for many years.

I was shocked by what she said, because my daughter is everything that I am not. In my eyes, she is as perfect as she was when I was blessed to give birth to her on November 27, 1999. She's very smart and articulate; she's everything that I longed to be and has everything that I longed to have when I was her age. She has long, thick hair; an average build; beautiful features; and soft, caramel-colored skin. She's talented, creative, outgoing, and has a wonderful sense of humor. How could she ever feel the same ugly feelings of inadequacy that I did when I was her age?

At that age, I felt like an alien. I was teased and called names because of my chocolate-colored skin and being big-boned, which is a soft way of saying heavy for my age. I felt that I had to prove my worth and intelligence in every fashion, whether to impress the teacher or make my parents proud, and I had to work on something that I knew I was good at in order to hold onto the sliver of self-esteem I had. But that's not my daughter's story; for her, beauty, intelligence, and good body structure are innate. Everything I struggled with seems to come to her with ease.

So I was shocked when in a casual conversation with her about the litany of things that had happened at school that day, she mentioned not doing as well as she could in a certain subject. Of course, I went into mommy mode, reassured her of how smart she was, and reminded her that she will have another chance to demonstrate her natural, God-given abilities. As I shrugged it off and waited to hear the next bullet point of her day, she said, "I wish I was as smart as Marsha (name changed for anonymity) in my class." From there, she went on to compare herself to yet another girl in her class, wishing she was as pretty as her and that her hair was as long as hers. In my daughter's view, both of those girls were perfect and had more advantages than she did. She felt inadequate, because she did not measure up to her view of them.

At that moment, I heard an internal, ear-piercing screech that reminded me of a four-car collision on a highway with enough metal flying to make the 5:00 news. In front of me stood four feet and three inches of ideal. She radiated the best of me and then some; yet she didn't know it. And judging by the lowered eyes and sullen look on her face, she didn't feel it, either. There in the kitchen, I saw my past and present self in her sad eyes, and the revelation hit like a bowling ball dropped on my foot. I couldn't ignore or hide the fact that my daughter, who had everything I had longed for as a child—long, thick hair; beautiful, light-colored skin; and unending creativity—felt that she was not enough.

A swarm of questions stirred in me, culminating into one that resounded in and gripped my heart: if she doesn't know now that she is all of these wonderful things, when will she know? Then the mirror reflected the same question to me: Melissa, when will *you* know? When will you stop doubting your self-worth and disavowing your birthright by comparing yourself to others, believing the lies of old, and living in the illusion that you are not who you are or where you should be in this life? When will you accept your own internal and external beauty, love who you are, and live every day like you love the person staring back at you in the mirror? And when will you grasp the evolutionary gift that you have been given—your entitlement to possess all that you need for this journey?

I had read every self-help book I could think of, listened to every positive-thinking tape advertised, and accomplished every goal that would make an outsider think I had the self-confidence of a dragon slayer. However, there in my kitchen, I came face-to-face with my mini-me who, despite her perfection, felt as abnormal as I did years before her conception. It was then that I realized I had to come back to who I was forty-plus years earlier when I came into this world as more than enough. Somehow, I had buried my birthright by allowing others to infiltrate my self-image with twisted lies, innuendos, and preconceived notions. I came with more than enough beauty, health, strength, love, intelligence, and joy, and I didn't need to spend a lifetime looking for it in self-help books, a man's arms, or other people's approval. I didn't need to walk around, carrying the burden that I was a work in progress, had to go through a process, and would one day find my way to a forced epiphany.

I held my daughter that day as if I were cradling her in my arms for the very first time and told her, "You are more than enough—just because you were born that way, not because you have to become enough, to learn to be enough, or to read a bunch of self-help books to convince yourself that you are capable of being enough." Because of who she was and because she originated from a supreme perfect Spirit that made her more than enough, she needed to claim her birthright courageously, confidently, and without apology. I told her to lift her head, look at all that her eight-year-old self was telling her, and know that she had all she needed to do her best, have the best, and be the best that she was meant to be.

I shocked myself when I unveiled this truth that lies within each and every one of us. It is a message that is encrypted in our DNA—one that I hope you will rediscover, dear reader, as I share my journey and offer you time-saving tips and encouragement as you continue yours. This book is not meant to be a self-help book with steps on how to become better at who and what you are. If you have picked it up for that purpose, you will be greatly disappointed, for I am not a self-help guru and do not aspire to be. But if you are looking to be inspired and rediscover your true self—your hidden core that wants to engulf your entire being—this is the book for you. It is meant to share with you my experiences, my inner conversations, and the wisdom I have gleaned from others along the way so that you do not have to waste your time looking for something you already have within yourself.

I hope it inspires you to step beyond what the world says you are—who you have come to believe you are—into a realization of who you were *made* to be and what you are *entitled* to have. I hope that it reaches that place in you where truth and beauty dance as an inseparable force awakening a brilliant self-awareness that radiates from every pore in your skin. I have faith that it will release in you a pool of joy, hope, and love that will be passed on to your children and their children to come.

I hope this book serves as a loving testament to you and your daughters that you can take through this lifelong journey. I hope that together, we can hold onto some of the *a-ha* moments, pearls of wisdom, and grains of grace that are sprinkled within these pages that might help us reestablish our sense of being. In this book lies my life-changing experiences, connections I have made with other women, and deep wishes for my daughter, who I hope will be strengthened by these words even after my journey ends.

I also hope that this book serves as a challenge for you to hold on to your true self and not allow any one person or circumstance to take you away from you. I hope that you will be inspired to hold on to the core of truth that you possess and the knowledge that you have what it takes to meet life's challenges head-on and to overcome them victoriously with yourself intact.

Along with some of my personal experiences, I share stories of other women who have gone through trials and struggles and conquered them through their faith and inner strength.

After each chapter is a summary of the most important points called "Embracing the Message." There you will also find a Scripture reflection that can be used as a devotional or to aid you in your personal study. (All Bible verses throughout the book were taken from the New International Version of the Bible unless otherwise noted.) Finally, on the last page of the chapter, you will find Journal Notes. These questions allow you to reflect and examine yourself in critical areas including self-esteem, self-acceptance, and self-love. The chapter in its entirety is to serve as a guide through your own personal discovery and revelation that you are divinely enough and more than capable of having all that your heart can hold.

If you are up to the challenge, let us journey to that place where all that you are abides. First, imagine yourself standing on a mountain with the dawn of a new day creeping into the sky behind you. As you look at the valley below, you pick up a bullhorn and shout to every self-doubting moment you have had, in front of every disappointment that has rocked your confidence, and before every person who has belittled you or who you have compared yourself to and have come up short, "I am divinely enough!"

It echoes from the valley, reverberates from the mountainside, and flows to your ears in the wind again and again. Capture the moment. Remember it as if it were part of your birth date. Log it into your memory so that you will recall it again as mindlessly as you would when asked your own name. This divine image is who you are—who you were created to be—and no one, nothing, no circumstance, and no event can ever change that!

Let us begin …

CHAPTER 1

Decide to Decide

My Story: Finding My Worth

I decided to pack.

I got a huge cardboard box, secured the bottom with packing tape, and filled it with some sweaters, sheets, and towels. Soon, the living room was stacked with different-sized boxes, some with writing on the sides that displayed their prior contents: Kellogg's, Dixie, and Tropicana. They were piled in corners and stuffed to the rim with pots, curtains, old papers, toys, and baby clothes. Each box was distinct in size and with different demarcations—*kitchenware* was scribbled at an angle on one; another read *bedroom stuff*, while yet another had *winter clothes* scrawled in black marker across the back.

Combined, the boxes symbolized the end of my ten-year marriage. I didn't want to accept it at the time. I told myself and my then husband that we needed a break—that I was taking the baby (and all our things) to Virginia to sort things out. I lied to myself and to him and said that I'd be back in six months, though I had sold the house, packed my things, and didn't really care where he was going to live. I needed to breathe. I needed to be whole again. I needed to get out of a toxic situation that had sucked everything I had to give. I was emotionally drained, mentally tired, and in survival mode. I had to flee or spiritually and mentally die.

It wasn't an easy decision for me to make, especially with a daughter who was barely two, still waddling around in diapers that sagged off her bottom. But it was a decision that had to be made, because the relationship with my husband had soured to the point that it threatened to damage my health and well-being. I had to leave, escape, and find a safe place to run. For me, packing brought clarity and purpose. It pointed to a direction on my mental compass. Each box brought confirmation that I was doing the right thing and gave me a reason to move toward something better and new.

I can't tell you specifically when my marriage started to decay, but the stench became unbearable when my husband moved into the back room and stopped talking to me. Before this, we had gone through the motions, pretended that everything would be all right, gone to a get-your-marriage-back-on-track retreat, talked about what we could do to fix it, worked on it for a few days, and then went back to business as usual—until I looked around one day and the relationship was as lifeless and useless as a corpse. He refused marital counseling, and I got tired of begging him to go with me.

I talked to, pleaded with, and cajoled him, but by this time, his heart was hardened, and his mind was made up about how things between us had to be. From his place of hurt, I deserved my punishment, which lasted almost six months. At the time, part of me believed he deserved to treat me like an unclean leper, as guilt had settled in, and remorse had taken its toll on my psyche for my part in the decay.

I became intimate with the feelings of rejection, isolation, and disappointment. The only thing that saved me from sinking into a cycle of depression was an inner belief that I was worthy of more. I did not deserve this. That inner knowledge was deeply rooted in my belief that I deserved to be loved, respected, and honored. After all, if God so loved the world that He sent His only son to die for me (John 3:16), then I must be worthy of something more than I was getting. All I did was react to a situation that I was put into without any forewarning or consideration. I stopped feeling sorry for myself and fretting over my maggot-infested relationship when one day, I saw my little one toddle her chubby thighs down the hall instinctively to find her father in the other bedroom. I knew then that something had to change.

I had two options: I could continue living like this, or I could do something about it. I had apologized. I had talked to my husband. I had prayed, cried, lost sleep, and stopped eating over this thing that was ripping our family to the core. I didn't know what would happen in the long run, but I knew what I did not want to happen to my child. I knew that I did not want her to grow up going from one bedroom to the next to find her parents, and I did not want to go through the remaining years of my life feeling exiled, powerless, and worthless in my own home. Somehow, I knew that I deserved more for myself and my child.

I knew that I had the ability to get more and be more—to be treated better, respected, and loved just because of who I was.

I decided to pack! I made a life-changing decision that transformed the scope of how I perceived myself and what I expected of myself. It was as if a light switch was turned on in a photographer's dark room, and all of the images that someone had taken of me and told me that I should be were instantly damaged. The catch was that I had to remake the pictures one at a time by believing in the simple fact that I am *divinely* enough. I am worthy of more than life could ever pay, and within me (and you), there is more than enough creativity, will, tenacity, and innate ability to give to this world and get through anything that life throws my (our) way.

We are divinely made and designed to overcome whatever emotional obstacles we face. Our bodies and minds are created to protect, renew, and replenish themselves. Why should we think that we are made to just crumble at the first problem or circumstance that does not initially go our way? Be grateful for who you are and what you have to offer life. Refuse to give up or back down from the challenge. Hold your head up high, and no matter where you are on this journey, know that you're going to make it, because you are made specifically to do just that.

Her Story: The Worthiness of a Woman

I shared my story with a former teacher a few years ago when she ended up questioning her worth as a woman. It was a morning like any other in a school of over 1,700 students—murmuring in the front office, little feet scampering to get to class, the audio hum of the PA announcement followed by the annoying late bell that resounded throughout the campus at its 8:05 cue. As one of the school administrators, I had to ensure that the morning ritual happened according to schedule.

There was nothing unusual or special about my agenda that day that suggested that I would have the evangelical moment that later transpired. Everything was redundant and routine, from the message slips of parent calls to return to the stack of disciplines in my inbox waiting for me from the afternoon before. But in the midst of the monotony, I received a call from the front office secretary letting me know that one of our teachers had called in sick. I responded with my rehearsed question, asking whether she had called for a substitute to carry out her pre-filed emergency lesson plans. That's when the secretary hesitated and changed the script, asking me to call the teacher, because the situation was serious and could not be knocked out by a shiny colored pill or chicken noodle soup.

Not knowing what to expect, I called the teacher to find out if she was okay, desperately wanting to get to the burning question: *Did you call for a sub?* The response on the other end was followed by sobs and an inaudible rambling about not wanting me to know. The teacher finally composed herself long enough to let me know how sorry she was for this and that she did not want this to happen. Before I could console her, she started speaking as quickly as one of the students trying to explain why he was sent to the office with a discipline.

The only lines that I could decipher were powerful enough to change the course of my planned day. She said that *he* had hit her several times. She explained that this man had pushed and punched her and left her cowering in the closet with her nine-year-old daughter. She said she got enough nerve to call the police and that he was arrested the previous night. Through the string of questions that rushed through her like water from a dam that had been irreparably broken, the one that resounded clearly to me was, *What am I going to do without him?*

I heard an internal four-car collision, and everything in my world came to an abrupt halt. Logic did not permit me to understand her question or conjure up an intelligent reply to it. Deeply saddened and stunned, I stepped out of my role as administrator and supervisor and went to her home to serve as an advisor and friend. I rushed over to her house as fast as my Chevy Cavalier could take me to lend a shoulder, hand, or whatever I could to help this teacher I knew to be calm, committed to students, passionate about her profession, and rational.

She always had a smile on her face that lit up any classroom and a spirit that reassured her students that they could achieve more than they expected. She taught middle school language arts, and she taught it well. With passion for the written language, she confidently guided her students through grammar rules, sentence structure, and syntax. I observed lessons in which she encouraged students to find their voice and use language to express themselves concisely, clearly, and creatively. Yet when she opened the door, she stood devoid of all of the tenets she had taught. Her pale, sunken face said more than her shaky words tried to express. She was a shadow of the woman I had seen on the school walkway the day before.

Displaying brokenness, loss, confusion, and shame, her eyes flitted back and forth as if trying to hold back the flood of tears just waiting for permission to run. As she motioned for me to come in and sit down in her spacious living room, she painted the picture that transpired the night before of a woman who was pushed, punched, and slapped for no reason other than the fact that a man was angry. She said when he finally left the house in a fury, she locked the door, called the police, turned out all of the lights, and hid in the closet with her confused and shaken daughter.

She recollected how she was afraid to open the door for the police and only did so when she saw the flashlight that beamed through her bedroom window. She told them and now me that he had done this before, that he had a bad temper, and that she did not want him to be arrested. Now that the police had arrested him and taken him to jail despite her wishes, she did not know if she would press charges. She didn't want anything to happen to him or for him to be mad at her. She gave me all the reasons why she thought he got angry enough to lay his hands on her "this time." She explained why she thought he punched and pushed her at other times. She cried, worried, stared blankly, cried, and worried some more.

She worried about what I thought of her, what his parents would say, and what her parents would think, because they told her not to take him back. What would her sister think about her? How would her daughter feel if she pressed charges? What would this do to her daughter? Would he be mad at her? Would he be all right in jail? Would she be able to live with herself if she pressed charges? Why did he do this … again?

These questions came from a wonderful person who loved children, wanted to return to school to get a graduate degree, and paid all of the bills while he worked as an artist who sold no paintings. She was co-owner on both of the cars and the two houses they shared. Her eyes were glazed over, and her eyelids were puffy from the now dried tears that had streaked down her face. She looked lost like a child who was abandoned in a busy mall—wide-eyed, awestruck, and not knowing which way to run or who to trust. She looked at me as if I had some answers to the barrage of questions crashing through her mind. She looked at me with all that she thought she had left in her and asked me what she should do.

As she talked to me, part of me wanted to hug her as an older sister would a younger sibling who had just gotten beaten up at school; the other part wanted to grab her arms, shake her to her senses, and then push her out the door, telling her not to come back until she stood up to the bully. I wanted to tell her, "Girlfriend, you need to decide to pack." But I couldn't, because she was not there yet. She did not believe that she was capable of moving on and thriving without him. She did not know in her heart who she was or that she belonged to someone greater than the man who hurt her.

She continued to give me all of the reasons she should take him back as she ran her fingers through her disheveled hair. In her reverie, I remembered when I had observed her teaching a lesson. She told the students that they had to find their voices by listening to what was inside of them all the time. She told them to be creative and to think of ways to tell their stories by helping the characters to solve the problem.

I recalled this for her, stressing the same words and phrases she used weeks before: *find your inner voice, listen to yourself, have confidence in your abilities to find a solution.* I told her that she deserved all the goodness that life had to offer and that she had the right to ask for and demand to be loved, respected, honored, and admired for the beautiful person she was and all the wonderful talents and gifts that she had to give. I told her that she had the right to believe that she had the fortitude and aptitude she needed to make it without him and that she did not have to be bothered with proving to anyone, least of all an abusive man, that she deserved more. She was in a situation that she had chosen to be in time and time again, but her choice did not have to be the legacy that she passed down to her daughter and future grandchildren.

I knew abuse wouldn't be the legacy that I passed on. Like her, I had been in a relationship that sucked me dry and left me doubting my self-worth, value as a person, and right to believe that I was more than what one man told me I was. I admit that I do not know what it is like to be physically abused. I also do not know what it is like to cower in a closet because your husband or boyfriend has become your assailant, but I am keenly aware of what it is to be emotionally and psychologically abused. I know what it's like to surrender your confidence and self-esteem in a relationship after you have been degraded, embarrassed, made to feel inept, emotionally spent, and naked, unsure of who you are, where you need to be, and where you came from. I do know what it is like to deal with the burden of not believing in yourself because you have lost every shred of your purpose, vision, and confidence. I know how it feels to be afraid of being yourself, because the person you live with has emotionally placed you in a closet to feel alone, ugly, and discarded.

Like her, once I was scared, confused, and searched for answers to questions that had questions as responses. Before I decided to pack, I was at one time just like her – a shadow of my true self, a ghost of who I used to be. I couldn't hear my inner voice, because it was muffled by the emotional pain. I couldn't see a future, because the here and now blocked it from my view. And I definitely couldn't find God, because my vision was blurred from shame, anger, and disappointment. When she looked at me with her eyes jetting back and forth, searching mine for answers, I could answer her with a fire of confidence and assurance that came from reclaiming my self-worth, because the emotional web she was now in was once my own.

I could hear the unasked question that many women live with daily: "Am I enough?" The question can come in the form of insecurity about our capabilities as women to maintain families and career; uncertainty of our worthiness to be loved affectionately, gently, and intimately; and denial of our right to be treated and respected like the divine goodness and beauty that we are and were created to be. John and Stasi Eldredge say in their book, *Captivating: Unveiling the Mystery of a Woman's Soul,* "Many women feel that, by the way. We can't put words to it, but deep down we fear there is something terribly wrong with us. If we were the princess, then our prince would have come. If we were the daughter of the king, he would have fought for us. We can't help but believe that if we were different, if we were *better,* then we would have been loved as we longed to be. It must be us."[1]

As they state, the problem is not us. We were born in the image of goodness, perfection, and beauty. God said everything He made in the beginning was good. When he made grass, herbs, and trees bearing fruit, He saw that they were good (Genesis 1:12).

1   John and Stasi Eldredge, *Captivating: Unveiling the Mystery of a Woman's Soul* (Nashville, TN: Thomas Nelson Publishers, 2005), 69.

When He made the stars, moon, and sun, He saw that they were good (Genesis 1:18). He made every creature in the sky and in the sea. Guess what? He saw that they were good (Genesis 1:21). He even blessed them and told them to be fruitful and multiply. In essence, He said they had a divine right to increase. He then made the creatures of the earth, from creepy-crawlers to beast like cattle. He thought they were good, too. (Genesis 1:25).

God finally made man in the likeness of His own image to rule over all that He had created. The Bible says when God looked at all that He had made, He saw that it was very good (Genesis 1:31). God rested, but He saw that His work was not complete. It was not enough! God took a rib from Adam to make Eve. God's work, which was at first "very good," was complete. Genesis 2 ends with, "Adam and his wife were both naked, and they felt no shame" (Genesis 2:25).

We, dear sisters, are Eve's daughters. We complete the creation that God made. We are the pinnacle of the splendor, beauty, and perfection that God made and thought was good. We are here for a divine purpose—to support and compliment all that God has created from the beginning. My heart is overjoyed that the first man and woman stood together before God, naked as they were created, and they were not ashamed. The woman did not feel less worthy of love than the man. She did not feel as if she was not enough of a woman before God. The Bible does not say that her eyes were lowered or that she cowered behind the man in the presence of God. No, she stood boldly next to him, as his partner, undaunted and proud of her place in God's presence. She knew she was divine in all her being. That was how she was created. That was who she was. And that is how God made us all to be.

My chest also puffs out with divine pride when I read about Jesus' life story. This perfect man was born from a woman. Now, if we were not divine and loved by the Most High, why would He have His own Son come through a woman? The Son of God could have come in any form He chose. But God chose for Him to come from the womb of a woman! She nurtured him, and He respected and listened to her. In Jesus' first miracle at the feast of Cana, His mother, Mary, came to Him and told Him that the guests were out of wine (John 2:3). Not only did Jesus honor the marriage between a man and a woman with His presence at a wedding, but He also listened to His mother and miraculously made wine from water just because she asked Him.

Don't forget the boldness of the woman who had a blood disease for twelve years. She unabashedly touched the hem of Jesus' garment in a crowd full of men so that she would be healed. He turned to her and said, "Take heart, daughter, your faith has healed you. And the woman was made whole from that moment" (Matthew 9:22). I love that she felt she had a right to touch Jesus! She felt worthy enough to reach out and get close to him.

When Simon's mother-in-law was sick with a fever and Jesus came to her and healed her (Mark 1:30), Jesus didn't question whether she was worthy of His time or healing. He just came, because she needed Him! I am excited to know that Jesus found us worthy of love, healing, and attention. Why should we not think that way about ourselves? Why should we let people beat us down (literally and figuratively) when we are worthy of so much more?

Our Story: Deciding to Embrace Our Worth

We must decide to accept who we are and know that we have all that we need to pull through any painful moments, difficult situations, or trying times along our journeys. We are everything that we have hoped for, expected, and wanted, as our possibility is built into our divine DNA. All we need to do is to take deep breaths and accept our worth. Don't question it or doubt that it exists. We need to reach within our hearts of love, tenderness, and tenacity and embrace our divinity, acknowledge it, and allow it to pour through our very beings.

All it takes is one decision—the decision to stay or leave; to love yourself or abandon yourself; the decision to accept your birthright or deny it. One decision leads to another, which leads to another; each choice dictates a habit that creates a belief that creates your life.

Decide, dear reader, that you are more than enough. Decide that you deserve the best that life has to offer, whether or not you are in a physically, emotionally, or verbally abusive situation or circumstance. You deserve more. You were built for more. You *must* believe that you will have more. Don't settle for less than all that you deserve.

> We need to reach within our hearts of love, tenderness, and tenacity and embrace our divinity.

It is your birthright to be treated with respect and dignity. You are a person of value who should receive all the love, happiness, peace, prosperity, and joy that life has to offer. Don't let anyone—male or female—take that right from you. Don't give it away, and don't trade it for a night of companionship or a cheap drink. Esau did this. He sold his birthright for some meat, because at that moment, he was hungry (Genesis 25:29–34). I equate that to him selling his worth for instant gratification and losing all that he was blessed to have. Don't sell yours. You are divinely enough as you are and deserve all the goodness life has to offer.

If you don't believe me, read John 10:10. Jesus Christ said, "I have come that you may have life, and that you may live it more abundantly." How can I have life more abundantly if I am broken, bruised, or beaten? How can I live abundantly if I feel bad about myself, someone else puts me down and keeps me down, or I deny the fiber of my being? How can I have life more abundantly if I am cowering in a closet, waiting for the police to arrive; if I am beaten every time the person I love gets mad; if I walk in a house where my husband does not talk to me; if I wait up at night, because my husband doesn't have the respect to call? I simply can't.

To have an abundant life, you must first decide that you deserve to have an abundant life. You must know in the core of yourself that you were born to have more than you need. You must believe that you are here for a reason other than to be dumped on, put down, ostracized, and rejected. Dear reader, you and I are destined for greatness, because we come from a lineage of love that we may not know or accept but is still there, reminding us that we do not have to accept less than what we deserve in this life.

Decide that you deserve what is your God-given right to have—respect for yourself, happiness in your home, peace in your heart, and overflowing love and abundance. Decide that no one should be allowed to steal from you your joy, hope, self-worth, laughter, or oneness with all that is good. Decide, dear reader, that you have more than enough to get you through the next minute in your life, the next chapter in life's book, and the next obstacle on your journey. You have what it takes in the core of your very being—no matter what your background, eye color, job description, or financial status. You were born with it, the universe sent you here to live it, and the source of goodness expects you to radiate it from within.

You must first decide that you will no longer resign yourself to being less than yourself or to being treated as less than the regal person you are. You don't have to read a three-hundred-page self-help book to do that; you do not have to wait in earnest to improve or go through some process to metamorphose into your regality. There are no audio tapes that you need to commit to memory; there is no chant that you have to say every day in front of the mirror. *Decide* that you will stand up for yourself and protect what you have naturally inherited—the right to be loved, be you, and have all the goodness life has to offer.

Decisions Made

I got a call from the teacher shortly after I left the school and took another job. She called to tell me that she made a few decisions. I wish that I could say that the teacher listened to my experiences and took my advice to empower herself so that she was no longer a victim in her own home. She gave me all of the reasons the man she lived with completed and needed her. She told me all the excuses as to why he just got angry at times and shared all of her strategies as to how she would work harder not to set him off. The more I listened, the more she explained why she couldn't, wouldn't, and shouldn't decide to accept her own inner strength and move beyond being a victim—a punching bag for a man who lacked sense and sensitivity.

Little did she know that she had made several decisions. She decided to stay with him, make excuses for him, continue to take what he dished out, and in this case, later take him back. She took him back even though her daughter was taken from her and put in a foster home, he and she had to go to separate counseling sessions, and he was incarcerated for a time and then released to await a court hearing for domestic violence charges.

I would like to say that she is the only woman who makes these types of decisions in these types of situations. I wish the statistics did not show that every nine seconds, a woman in the United States is assaulted or beaten.[2] Globally, one in three women are abused, and on average, abused women will return to their abusers six to eight times.[3] Psychiatrists and therapists have tried for years to explain why some women make the decision to stay in these types of situations ranging in terms that all seem to be summed up with the word *syndrome*.

I am sensitive to these women (and in some cases, men) who are in abusive situations and because of finances, upbringing, and social shackles do not decide to break free. They get caught in a downward, confusing spiral of fear, self-hatred, lack of self-esteem, and hopelessness. I do know that the source of love that created us did not give us the Spirit of fear, but that of power, love, and a sound mind (2 Timothy 1:7). We were born from a source of love that imparted in us peace and wholeness—not for

2   "Domestic Violence Statistics," last modified January 26, 2012, http://domesticviolencestatistics.org/domestic-violence-statistics.

3   "Why Women Stay," last modified March 29, 2013, http://letswrap.com/dvinfo/whystay.htm.

someone to slap around, abuse, and misuse. This same source gave us the power and ability to choose and decide. We can decide to change our situations in a quick second. Marriage, divorce, birth, and sometimes death are all life-changing moments that happen because we decide. We decide to say "I do," "I love you," "I will leave," and "I will stay." We surround those words with reasons and intentions to implement our decisions. But the core of it all is that we decide.

Instead of deciding to stay in an unhealthy situation for herself and her daughter, she had to first decide that she deserved more. She had to know within herself that she was more than enough as a human being, woman, mother, and girlfriend. She had to grasp this painful point in her life as an opportunity to regain what stolen from her but also something that she had willingly given away. She had to decide in that very moment that life was a divine gift and that in it lay all of the answers she sought. Each day, she could begin anew, knowing that life would offer the healing and answers that she so desperately sought.

Our connection ended a year after I bumped into her at a department store. She was exiting as I was entering. She told me that she and the man who beat her had gotten married. Like a blushing bride, she showed me her ring and told me her new last name. She explained how much she loved him and that she believed he was sorry for what he'd done. She avoided eye contact and made an excuse to leave what was now an uncomfortable encounter. I wished her the best and reminded her that she had every right to happiness. It was up to her to decide that she would not settle for anything less.

As she scurried to her car, I turned into the store and

remembered what my grandmother always had said: there are two things for certain in this life. You are born alone, and you will die alone—in between is your life. No matter the circumstances of your birth—whether you came here deliberately or by surprise, whether you were born poor or rich, black or white, tall or short, thin or plump, via c-section or natural birth—you came as a human being designed by a higher source of goodness and love. She also told me, "Melissa, you were created for a great purpose that only you can fulfill." I had to realize that all of this was in my makeup; I had to decide to nurture it and let it blossom from my core. Each day, I live to protect it with all that I am and know that I am worthy of all the love that this world has to offer! After all, as a woman, I am the pinnacle of God's creation. In me, His creation is complete.

It's that simple—in between birth and death is your life. You make the decision how to live it and how you will be treated. I hope and pray that you decide that you deserve the best, because you come from the best. I hope that you decide to hold true to who you are as a worthy child of the Creator. When you decide that you are worthy just because that's how you were created to be, you will be well on your way to claiming the power you have within that has been there from the very beginning of your essence. In that one decision, dear reader, you will shine like the miracle that you are!

EMBRACING THE MESSAGE

Deciding to Decide

🕊 *Decide* to find your voice, listen to what's inside of you, think of creative ways to solve problems, believe in yourself, and have confidence in your abilities.

🕊 *Decide* to make a difference in your circumstance. You are born alone, and you will die alone—in between is your life.

🕊 *Decide* to hold on to your worth. You are a person of value who should receive all the love, happiness, peace, prosperity, and joy that life has to offer. Don't let anyone—male or female—take that right from you. Don't give it away or trade it for a night of companionship or a cheap drink.

🕊 *Decide* that you will stand up for yourself and protect what you have naturally inherited—the right to be loved, the right to be you, and the right to have all the goodness life offers.

🕊 *Decide* to shine like the miracle that you are!

Scripture Reflection

"I have come that you may have life, and that you may have it more abundantly" (John 10:10).

Journal Notes: Deciding to Decide

Find your quiet place. (My quiet place is melting in a tub of hot water with soft music playing in the background. I light candles and burn incense.) Read these questions, and reflect on them. Let them sink into your mind and heart, but do not write anything down until you're ready. That may be the same day or later in the week.

1. What decision do you need to make in your life that is holding you back from your true calling as a worthy woman of God?

2. In what areas in your life have you made a decision to do nothing just to avoid doing something?

3. What conversation do you need to have with someone that you have been putting off?

4. What lies have you told yourself about your situation? What is the truth?

5. Think of a time when you felt powerless. What were some of the emotions that you felt?

6. How did you reclaim your power? (If you are still in a powerless situation, who do you plan to talk to in order to get help?)

7. Think of a time when you have felt powerful. What decisions led up to that moment?

8. What was the most defining message for you from this chapter? How will you implement it in your life?

Remember: Decide from your divine place of knowing what makes you the powerful and lovely person that you are.

CHAPTER 2

Love Yourself for Yourself

It was one of those days taken out of a horror novel. I stared at the pouring rain from my car window. The streetlight made the droplets look like transparent nails spiking down from the sky. They make an unnerving sound as they hit my blurred windshield, preventing me from seeing the car ahead. I carefully plodded along on the sleek street that looked more like a slippery slide at an adventure park than a tar road. Looking desperately for the blue and white hospital sign shown on the bulletin board in every driver's manual, I crawled sheepishly at five miles per hour to the dismay of the honking driver behind.

It seemed that everything that could possibly go wrong that night did, from me leaving the house late, to the gas gauge reading nearly empty. I kept telling myself that I should not have come, but a deep sense of obligation forced me into the car on less than an eighth of a tank of gas. Ahead, the large white neon sign of the hospital beckoned me. I found parking on the busy New

York street. I slammed the car door shut and ran across four lanes of traffic with the wind blowing my jacket open and my now broken black tote umbrella in tow. I flew into the administration building and was given directions that led me on an unplanned tour of the west wing.

Searching desperately for assistance, I looked at my watch. If it could talk, it would have said, "Girl, what in the world are you doing here? You only have ten more minutes before visiting hours are over." A yellow hospital bucket proved to be the answer I was looking for, because around the corner, the custodian was mopping the floor. All I heard him say was to go somewhere to the right down the hall. As my wet clothes drooped off my body, I traipsed and sloshed down the hall to an arrow that directed me to another corridor. At the end of that corridor, there was a closed door with a small, scratched Plexiglas window. I tried to open the worn brass handle, but the door was locked.

Through the window, I could see a patient on the other side of the bolted door walking stoically down the hall. His hair was unkempt, and he twirled some of it through his fingers. Standing there, he seemed to be in a trance as he rocked back and forth like the timed pendulum on a grandfather clock. Another patient on the right was slouched forward in a wheelchair outside her room. Her socks were rolled down to her ankles, and one of her bedroom slippers was hanging partially off her foot that was on the metal support. There was yet another patient further down the hall wringing his hands and then flinging them while stepping back and forth in place. I stood for a moment in awe and disbelief as I looked at the black plastic sign on the door that prevented me from entering that part of the corridor. In white numbers and letters, the sign listed the visiting hours for the mental health facility and the number for the nurses' station in case of emergency.

It hit me that my girlfriend was on the other side of the door. I had come to visit her after her mother had said her youngest daughter had had a nervous breakdown, but I did not expect to see the reality that unfolded before me. I'm not sure what I had expected to see. I had been to hospitals before, and the patients I visited were always in comfortable rooms and able to speak with me. They complained of the food or the fact that they couldn't get any rest because of the constant noise and always told me how much they wanted to go home. I had been in the hospital, too, when I delivered my daughter. How bad could it be?

Nowhere in my wildest imagination had I thought a nervous breakdown equaled disorientation and disconnection to reality. Somewhere in my naiveté, I thought it equaled bed rest and self-reflection time. Maybe if I had thought about it clearly, I would have come to a conclusion that reflected the reality in front of me. But how could I accept that thought? My childhood girlfriend was behind those doors. We were next door neighbors who had played jump rope together, pigtails flying in the air. We played school with the dolls lined up in rows and shared our goals and dreams, from her wanting to be a doctor to me wanting to be a teacher.

As I turned to leave, I was in a stupor and walked stoically back down the hall. I don't remember leaving the hospital or even how I got to my car. As I sat in the driver's seat, I stared at the rain as it reflected from the streetlight like shards of glass hitting the windshield, making a constant rushing sound. The reality of the moment hit me hard as I laid my head on my hands that gripped the steering wheel. Like my car, I was stuck in the moment without any motivation to move on.

My girlfriend was in a mental ward—but the patient could have been me. She was only two years older than I. Like me, she had done everything right. She went to college, got married, bought a house, had a good job, and had a daughter a few years older than mine. We had spoken about our marriages. We had prayed together. We had shared ideas and thoughts. How could this have happened to her? Maybe it could happen to me. Her mother had said she just snapped. My friend's mother told her to slow down, take time for herself, not run herself ragged, and look in the mirror at the wonderful person she was. Her mother told her to put herself first, love herself for herself, and stop worrying about her husband's late nights and harsh words—but her daughter was still in a mental facility.

I finally cranked my car and headed toward the interstate. I had to get a hold of myself. I did not want to be one of those patients on the other side of the door, twisting my hair, slouching in a wheelchair, wringing my hands, or rocking back and forth with no sense of time or awareness of place. The patient could have been me. My life flashed in front of me. Like a movie, I saw the arguments with my husband, late nights up with the baby, and stacks of papers that I had to grade. It could have been me.

I felt the heaviness of my life from the unhappiness I experienced in my marriage, rejection I felt as a wife, and failure I felt as a teacher who was unable to reach her students. It could have been me, but it wasn't; and since it wasn't, I was determined that it wouldn't be. I would take hold of my life, take it easy on myself, and love me for me.

On the long ride home, I realized that I did not want to snap. I did not want to lose touch with who I was or my sense of reality. I did not want to be on the verge of mental purgatory, where no one could reach me. I can't tell you that a wave of love flooded me or that I had any type of "Eureka!" experience. But when I walked in my front door, drenched, without an umbrella, and cold, I was not the same woman who had left.

Life is transient. One day, you're sane, and the next, you're not. In one moment, you're in touch with reality, and the next, you're in another world. One day, you hate yourself and your life, and the next, you're learning to love the beautiful being that you are. In an instant, things, people, and circumstances can change, but the love you have for yourself *must* remain constant. You and I *must* remember to always love ourselves, keep ourselves in the forefront of our minds, make it our daily mission to be good to ourselves, and give ourselves all that we give to others—and then some.

How do you do this when life is full of demands that drain your energy, attention, and focus? As the *Nike* commercial says, "Just do it!" You have to. There are no other options or choices. You have a nonnegotiable contract with all the goodness on this planet. You deserve to love you! Although we'd like to believe that loving others more than we love ourselves makes us valuable and worthwhile, it doesn't. Loving ourselves and then loving others makes us invaluable and gives us the energy and strength to live with purpose. Taking time out for ourselves to honor who we are and the fact that we are here is the ultimate way to show others that we love them, because we want to be healthy and sane in order to be of value to them.

A few years ago, I would have read that last statement and shrugged it off, because I would know that the writer had no clue about my life. She would not know that I had a ton of deadlines to meet, a household to run, a daughter to raise, a marriage to fix, lesson plans to create, a part-time job in the evenings to rush to, and the other to-do items on my list that was as long as a city block.

If you are like I was, then you need to hear this: a healthy young woman was doing all of the things that I did and more. She *was* the daughter of one of my mother's friends and not much older than I was at the time. This young woman was divorced, raising her children, working, and going to nursing school. One evening, my mother called to tell me that her friend's daughter was dead. Apparently, the young woman came home that evening, and after her nightly routine, she sat at her table to study. Her two teenage children found her slouched over there, dead from a heart attack.

After the funeral, her ex-husband moved into the house and reclaimed custody of the children. Her life was over. Her to-do list for the next day remained undone. I wonder if she ever took time out to get a check-up. I wonder if she took a day off from work for a "Do Me Day to pamper herself. I wonder if she took time to talk and laugh with her friends or go for a stroll around the park by herself just to breathe in the fresh air.

She could have been me. Her fate could have been mine—or even yours. If you're like me or her, you also have a routine. As a single mother, I often rush home to get my daughter to go to dance. We come back home to do homework and study together for her tests. While we do homework, I usually eat, wash dishes, make lunch, and take care of the dog. I always look at the clock and wonder where the time has gone. On a good night, we're in the bed by 8:30 p.m. with the expectation of starting the same routine the next day. She could have been me.

I've learned the hard way that you must take time out and love yourself. Restore yourself. Give back to yourself. Slow down, and enjoy the breaths that you take. I force myself to wake up at 5:00 in the morning to give myself time to replenish, reflect, and restore what was taken from me the day before. During my time, I exercise with my now memorized cardio videos, pray, and then mediate on the day ahead. In the evenings, I take a hot bath with instructions to my daughter: *this is Mommy's time.* I light my candles; play Luther, Whitney, or India Arie; and slip away in the warmth of the gentle water, letting the melody and Calgon's fragrance take me away.

I've learned to carve time out to get my hair done regularly, and if I'm in the mood, I get a manicure and pedicure, too. I deserve this. You deserve it. Life is too challenging and short not to carve time out for you. Stop hurrying your life away with routines that usually don't include doing something for yourself. Give yourself permission to stop and to love you—all of you, every wrinkle and extra curve. Love yourself. Take time out for yourself. You're going to be stopped one way or the other if you keep ignoring yourself. Take time to love yourself, celebrate yourself, and be proud of who you are.

> **Give yourself permission to stop and to love you—all of you, every wrinkle and extra curve. Love yourself.**

Loving You

How do you love yourself? You must first embrace the person you are. Face the reality that is before you, and if need be, say the Serenity Prayer a couple of times: "Lord, grant me the serenity to accept the things that I can't change, the courage to change the things that I can, and the wisdom to know the difference." Leave worry, fear, and rejection at the back door, and walk out the front with self-confidence, self-respect, and self-admiration.

I recently attended a seminar on relieving stress. The conference room was filled with women of all ages and ethnic backgrounds. The speaker was full of vigor and excitement. She encouraged a Baptist church-like atmosphere and told us that we could shout "Amens" and "Alleluias" if and when we wanted. The charge in the room was electric until she got to the question, "How many of you do something special for yourself on a continual basis?" My hand shot up like a firecracker full of energy and purpose. When she called on me, I felt as if the entire room turned to look at me. I ranted a list of things that I do for myself, including manicures, pedicures, getting my hair done, and massages. I don't do those things every week, but I make sure my hair is tight, my nails are clean, and my toes don't look like something from a Jurassic Park close-up.

What hit me like a splash of ice water was that when the speaker asked other women what they did for themselves, they searched for things to say and did not have the same energy or enthusiasm that I had had in my response. Some responded that they went to dinner with the in-laws or had movie nights with the kids. How is that doing something just for you? I felt very selfish in my response, as if I had disobeyed the eleventh commandment for women only: *Thou shalt not pamper thyself.* I could feel my body melt like heated gelatin in the hardback chair, and I sank in shame!

But then my sister-girlfriend's voice boomed in my mind as the speaker encouraged women to take time out for self. Her voice faded like a hum in the background while my inner voice took the microphone. It said, "You better sit yourself up in that seat, girl. You have nothing to be ashamed of! You've come a long way from thinking that you were the last thing deserving love on this planet to embracing your right to have the best that life has to offer. Now, sit yourself up, and hold your head up high. You are a wonderful mother, daughter, sister, and friend, and you owe it to yourself to love yourself and show yourself how deserving you are of being pampered, taken care of, and replenished in body, mind, and spirit."

The shocking thing about this whole experience is that most of the women in the room did not reveal that they put themselves first or that they took time out for themselves. I felt some regret over doing just the opposite instead of being proud of it. The bottom line is this: how do you see yourself? What do you see when you look in the mirror—a queen, a tired mother, a happy wife, a dutiful daughter? When you see your future, what do you see? A house and a white picket fence, a mansion, a condo by the lake, a room in a basement? If you are looking for a man, do you see a candlelight dinner with a warm-hearted gentleman, a walk on the beach with a hunk of a man

> When you see yourself as yourself, you not only see all the possibilities that are available to you, but also *know* that you deserve them.

like Dwayne "The Rock" Johnson, a movie with someone who makes you laugh, or a hamburger at the corner grease spot with jobless Joe? Do you see yourself in a pickup truck with you sitting in the back, in a new Lamborghini with a sunroof, or on a rusted, busted bicycle for two? When you see yourself as yourself, you not only see all of the possibilities that are available to you, but also *know* that you deserve them.

The song *What the World Needs Now is Love* written in 1965 by Hal David and music composed by Burt Bacharach begins with the lyrics, "What the world needs now is love sweet love. It's the only thing that there's just too little of." Some of us can change the words to "what I need now is self-love, self-love. It's the only thing that I have too little of." How can we love others if we don't first love ourselves? If we do love ourselves, then why do we not take care of ourselves? We have a responsibility to nurture the love within by taking care of our mental, physical, and spiritual health. It's not enough to say that you love yourself. Love is action. First John 3:18 says, "Our love must not be a thing of words and fine talk. It must be a thing of action and sincerity." My question to you is this: what do you do for yourself? What do you say to yourself? What do you hope for yourself?

Clearly, I'm not referring to self-absorbed love. I'm not talking about the mothers who spend hundreds of dollars on their hair and nails but don't have a carton of milk in the refrigerator for their children. I'm not talking about wives who love themselves and their careers so much that family nights do not include them. I'm referring to a balanced and harmonious love with priorities. You cannot say you love yourself when you take care of house and home, work two jobs, and are stressed out to the point that you snap at your loved ones. You cannot say you love yourself when everything is taken care of, yet the bags under your eyes are so dark that you look like you are related to raccoons. I'm talking about the type of self-love that remembers that you are important in the midst of it all; that you are a priority, just like the children and your husband; that time spent alone is just as valuable as time spent with the family; that loving yourself does not mean that you must feel guilty, ashamed, or embarrassed about your choices to stay healthy, sane, and at peace.

During times when you are quiet and alone, love shows up and embraces you. During those times, our loving Father caresses us and fills us with a love so deep that we can't help but love ourselves. When you claim time for yourself, you invite Him to love you in the way that you need it. He whispers, "I love you as you are. Accept my love. Love yourself as I've created you to be." If you don't believe me, read John 13:34, John 15:12, Romans 5:8, and Romans 8:39. I could go on and on with references of God telling us in His own words, *"I love you!"*

Self-Hate

I wish that I could puff my chest out, brag, and say that I've always loved myself and accepted God's love for me. I wish that I could skirt around the fact that I have hated myself and have not been my best caretaker and friend. Since I can't, I'll tell you the first time I recall hating myself—when I was teased about the color of my skin. I was in the fourth or fifth grade when two boys from my class teased me mercilessly about being dark-skinned. It was the first time I felt something was wrong with me. I wished from that very moment that I was light-skinned like my mother. I asked her if my skin color would change. Bless her heart; she said that when she was a child, her skin was dark, and she lightened up as she got older. Little did I realize at the time that my mother was probably dark as a child growing up in the sunny island of Panama, and when she came to the United States she no longer had an island tan!

Nevertheless, I grew up with a complex and hated the skin that I was in. Then my parents got divorced, and somewhere along the way, I picked up the idea that everybody but me should be happy. If you believe this, you put others before yourself, make sure that everyone has something you want but refuse to give it to yourself, and give of yourself to the point of exhaustion. You also suffer when you can't say no, always volunteer, and never taking time out for self.

My self-hatred had no outward signs. On the surface, it seemed that I was the most confident, well-adjusted young woman you could ever meet. If you looked at my accomplishments in school, you would never be able to see any of my self-hatred symptoms. But they were there, just lying menacingly dormant.

When I met my husband, I wondered what on earth he saw in me. After all, he was light-skinned and muscular. What could I have that would attract him to me? My condition got worse during the course of my marriage. If you asked me then if I had self-hatred, I would have denied any of its obvious symptoms. My family told me to slow down and take time for myself. Like a foreigner in a new country, I did not understand any of those words.

I saw the movie *The Passion of the Christ,* and like almost everyone who has seen it, the film left me with another perspective of the crucifixion. Whatever you believe about Jesus Christ, no one can deny that He existed on this planet. He was a prophet who believed that He came to make things new. According to the gospels and other historical texts, He preached about loving one another and said it is the greatest commandment of all (Mathew 22:36–40).

I began to think about how much Jesus suffered for His belief and the love He must have had for us and for God. I listened to a sermon on this movie, and the minister said that love died on the cross at Calvary. I thought of the long hours He suffered. I thought of the things He must have thought of as He was abandoned, humiliated, whipped, and then nailed to wood. I imagined Him thinking of His purpose, and in His divinity, thinking about all of the people who would come after Him who He would save just because of His death. Their names came flooding through His mind, and it gave Him strength to endure. In the nine hours He hung on the cross, I believe my name crossed His mind, and that as gospel artist Donny McClurkin says, "He did it just for me." If He loved the world (me) so much that He would humble himself and die an excruciating death (Philippians 2:8), then why do I not love myself? If He paid the price for me on Calvary already, as the gospels say, then why do I feel that I am not worthy of love?

I can't tell you that my life changed instantly. But when I concentrate on the love that was nailed on the cross centuries before I was even thought of, how can I not love myself? During the Civil Rights Movement, Dr. Martin Luther King, Jr. said in his famous "I Have A Dream" speech,

> I have a dream that one day my four little children
> will one day live in a nation where they will not
> be judged by the color of their skin but by the
> content of their character. I have a dream today. I
> have a dream, that one day down in Alabama, with
> its vicious racists, with its governor having his lips
> dripping with interposition and nullification; one
> day right there in Alabama, little black boys and
> little black girls will be able to join hands with little
> white boys and little white girls. I have a dream
> today.[4]

If Dr. King loved his children and this nation enough to want things to be better, believe that things could be better, and risk his life for things to get better, then why should we not believe the same? Dr. King didn't know me from Adam. But if he thought that I am worthy enough of the right to be treated fairly, then why should I not believe the same about myself? Why should I not think that I deserve more, am more, should have more, and should love myself more?

We are on this planet for a brief period of time. The saying "Here today, gone tomorrow" holds true when we lose those who are dear to us. Every time we put ourselves last and do not take time for ourselves, we waste an opportunity to give ourselves the lives and experiences that we deserve. Every time we believe lies about ourselves, we waste a moment to give ourselves the love we need.

When a baby is born, she needs love. Volunteers go to hospitals and hold abandoned babies for hours, because the infants need it

---

4   Martin Luther King, (1963, August). *I Have a Dream.* Speech presented at Civil Rights March, Washington, D.C.

for their development. Research shows that newborn babies will die if they are not held and shown love. What does that mean for us? How do we operate without love? How do we cope with not loving ourselves? We shouldn't. We were made from the source of love. Love came and died for us, and we should remember that we are more than worthy to give love to ourselves. This means taking time out for ourselves, feeding ourselves well, taking care of our physical bodies with exercise and rest, and thinking about ourselves with loving thoughts and words.

> Every time we put ourselves last and do not take time for ourselves, we waste an opportunity to give ourselves the lives and experiences that we deserve.

Love yourself for yourself, dear reader! Love who you are, what you are, and who you will come to be. Love the fact that you are here. Love that you came from love. Love your faults and flaws, because they make you unique. Love the skin that you're in. Love your shape and size. Love your weight; it makes you who you are. Love your health, and keep it balanced. Love your challenges, because they make you stronger. Love your personality, voice, walk, talk, and laughter, and do not reject them, as they are all a part of the lovely you. If you don't know how to begin to love yourself for yourself, start by not putting yourself down, not criticizing your flaws, and demanding that others respect you by how you treat yourself.

Love Is Respect

A former student seemed to have everything going for her. She was blessed with brains and beauty. She dressed in tight-fitting blouses, and her shorts were always a few sizes too small. I often sent this seventh-grader to the office to call home for a change of clothing for dress code violation. One day, she was upset that she had to wear a large school shirt to cover her revealing blouse that she and her mother had bought the day before. A conversation she had in the hallway with her other classmates spilled over into my classroom. Her attitude and slamming books on the desk forced me to address her dress code blues.

I turned around and said, "Close your books. We're going to have a discussion about self-respect." My reading class turned into an Oprah Winfrey-style talk show. I made sure the young ladies knew that revealing clothes do not equate to self-respect; that attention from a boy does not mean that he likes or loves you; and that self-respect and self-love are inward and must be reflected in how they carry themselves, speak, and treat others. I made sure the young men knew that they owed the young ladies respect and should treat them the way they would want their mothers and sisters to be treated by other young men.

I'm not sure where many young women get the idea that they have to be seductive in order to be loved or worthy of respect. We can blame society and the media for its negative images of women, starting from the music videos with scantily-dressed women to the soap operas with women pining over married men. We can also blame family history and trace a woman's lack of self-respect to the way her father treated her and her mother when she was growing up. Whoever or whatever we blame does not negate the fact that many young girls believe that self-love is directly connected to how a man feels about how she looks or how she should behave.

I've worked with many young girls as a youth leader and public school teacher, and I am saddened by the distorted belief that some young girls have about themselves. Self-respect is taught. A young lady learns self-respect from those around her and images and messages she *allows herself to believe.* I don't want my daughter to ever be defined by what another person—especially a man—thinks of her. She should have enough confidence in who she is as a person to know that she can be just as attractive in a business suit as she can be in a swim suit. I want her beauty to shine from within because of the love she has for herself and the self-awareness that she is somebody special just because of who she is, not because of who or how someone wants her to be.

Self-respect comes from loving yourself enough to know that you deserve love, because you are love, and you give love to yourself. No one has to love you for you to love who you are. No one has to approve of you before you can approve of yourself. Sure, as children, we look for acceptance and approval from our parents and other adults. We look for it in terms of school grades, notes sent home, or nods from our moms and dads. But as we mature into adults, we must transition from needing someone else's approval to needing our own. We must move from seeking someone else's respect to knowing that self-respect is sufficient. "When I was a child, I spoke like a child, I thought like a child, I reasoned like a child; but when I became a man I put away childish things" (1 Corinthians 13:11, KJV).

When you respect yourself, others have to do the same, because in the nature of self-respect, there is no room for disrespect. When you respect yourself, you demand respect from others. You do not associate with people or situations that are disrespectful to you. You honor yourself; therefore, where you are is always honorable. You are at peace with yourself; therefore, where you are, there is peace. You have the bar set at self-respect, so you walk with your head up; you speak with confidence; and you dress to capture your own attention, admiration, and love. Your clothes say, "I know who I am, but I don't have to reveal everything I've got."

Love Is Patient

Love is also patient. Loving yourself means taking the time to get to know yourself. It means giving yourself a break and laughing at your mistakes instead of always putting yourself down. Love is patient and knows that it takes time for growth and development. Those who love to garden know what I'm talking about. If you love your garden, you know that there are seasons, and it takes time for certain plants, trees, and flowers to grow. Tulips and daffodils come up every spring, but daisies come up later in the summer. These plants are called perennials; they come up year after year. You have to wait for them, but they blossom in their season.

Dedicated gardeners who love their gardens give them time. They nurture their gardens. They trim the hedges that need trimming; beautify and groom them; take time out to assess their gardens' needs for development and growth; and painstakingly pluck the weeds, careful not to pull the plants, so that the beauty of their gardens can radiate through. Gardeners are patient, because they love every aspect of their gardens, and their dedication shows in the flowers and plants that blossom and grow.

You are a garden. You are made up of all of the beauty that nature can give. Be kind to and patient with yourself. Take time to find out what you need. Maybe you need more rest in your schedule, or maybe you need a brief getaway. Love yourself enough to be patient with who you are and what you need to be outstanding, amazing, and above the rest. We are patient with our customers, children, spouses, and friends. Why are some of us so impatient with ourselves?

I am amazed at how patient Jesus was with all those around Him. I would have lost it with somebody, but not Jesus. After Lazarus died, Jesus said to His disciples that Lazarus was only asleep. Of course, His disciples didn't understand and ignorantly answered, "Lord, if he's sleep, he shall do well" (John 11:12, KJV). These men were with Jesus when He brought a child back from death with the simple phrase "Talitha cumi (Girl, arise)" (Mark 5:41). They saw Him open the eyes of the blind, heal the sick, cast out demons, feed thousands with a boy's lunch, calm a storm, and walk on water. I would have had no more patience with them, but Jesus did. The Bible simply says, "Then said Jesus unto them plainly, Lazarus is dead" (Luke 11:14, KJV). He didn't call them names or chastise them. He said, lovingly and patiently, "Let me explain what I mean, since you don't understand." If He could have such patience with them, why do we not have patience with ourselves?

Jesus was also patient with the crowds who came to hear Him speak and see Him perform miracles. Several places in the New Testament record Jesus' compassion on them (Mark 6:34, Matthew

14:14) My favorite passage says, "And seeing the multitudes, he had compassion on them; because they were distressed and lying like sheep that have no shepherd" (Matthew 9:36, KJV). I love this depiction of Jesus' patience and compassion, because He was tired. He had just gotten news that his cousin, John the Baptist, had been beheaded. Jesus wanted to get away, reflect, and possibly mourn. But when He saw the crowds, His love, compassion, and patience were so profound that He had them all sit on the mountain side and fed five thousand people. He listened, prayed, and taught with patience and love.

The disciple John summed it up best in his letters to Corinth: "Love is patient; love is kind and envies no one. Love is never boastful, nor conceited, nor rude; never selfish, not quick to take offense" (1 Corinthians 13:4) If love is patient, then be patient with yourself. Know that as a woman, you will have good days, when all your hormones are marching to the same beat, and days when they're not. Be kind to yourself on those days. On other days, know that you will make mistakes just because you are human. Take a deep breath. Embrace the love in and around you. Then allow yourself to be fully human, and patiently give your femininity the tender loving care that it needs.

Love Is Restoration and Forgiveness

Love is also restoration. It's taking time for yourself to be your true self. It is restoring what was depleted and lost. Restoration could be in the form of rest or just letting go. Restoration could also be in the form of self-forgiveness. If you carry baggage from your past, leave it at the door, and walk away from it. Drop that image of yourself, and replace it with a loving, gentle reflection of the love staring at you in the mirror.

It doesn't matter who you were before or what you did. What matters is the here and now. Who are you in this moment? You are simply love. You have enough love in your very being to radiate from inside. Tap into that love. Embrace it, and become the sign of love that you are. You may have to forgive yourself for making mistakes. You may have to let go of disappointment over gaining another five pounds after eating the whole six-layer carrot cake with whipped cream. Whatever you need to do to erase the slate for yourself, do it—and do it now.

I'm very glad that the Bible tells of the story of the woman who was going to be stoned to death for adultery (John 8: 3-11). That sister had it bad. She was sleeping around with other people's husbands, and the whole town knew about it! Her accusers came to Jesus and said that they caught her in the act of adultery. She was guilty and had eyewitnesses who could testify to her sin.

Jesus stooped down and drew on the ground, as if He had not heard them! He seemed unconcerned that this woman had sinned! Then Jesus stood up and said to them, "Let him who is without sin cast the first stone." Again, he stooped down and wrote on the ground. None of them could throw a stone at her, because they all had sinned. When the accusers left, Jesus then turned to the woman (who I imagine was huddled in shame) and asked, "Woman, where are your accusers?"

She replied, "They have gone."

Jesus replied with powerful words that you need to hear as much as she did at the time: "Then, I find no fault in you." How awesome is it to know that perfection walking in the body of Jesus said to a guilty adulterous woman, "Neither do I find fault in you. Go and sin no more"? I get excited when I hear that story! The perfect being—God in the flesh—said, "I find no fault in you." No matter what I or you have done, Jesus says, "I find no fault in you. I forgive you. You are whole in my sight. I have paid the price for your sin." Why do you walk around with the baggage of unforgiveness? Forgive yourself, and move into the love that you are!

You may remember the story about the prodigal son (Luke 15:11-32). He disrespected his father by telling him that he wanted his inheritance immediately and did not want to wait. He took his father's money and splurged on wild living. When he spent all his money, he was hungry and riddled with shame. The Bible says that when he came to himself, he realized that his father's pigs ate better than he did. He rushed home to his father, who was waiting for him! He told his father that he was not fit to be his son and would be a servant if he could only come home.

The father told his servants to have a feast in his son's honor and get him the best robes. He forgave his son and welcomed him back with open arms, saying to his eldest jealous son, "We had to celebrate and be glad, because this brother of yours was dead and is alive again; he was lost and is found" (Luke 15:32). I love imagining the smile on his father's face. He must have been full of joy and love, knowing that his son was home safe and sound. It's a story of forgiveness—the forgiveness of others and the forgiveness of self. Restore yourself, love yourself, and be patient with who you are—a garden full of radiant beauty created from love.

Dedication to Loving Yourself

My hope for you is that you dedicate yourself to loving yourself every day for as long as you live. Make a commitment to yourself that you will be patient enough to listen to yourself. Take time to pamper yourself, respect yourself, and forgive any faults or shortcomings you may have. Believe that you are from a source of love and can only reflect that love, because it is in you.

As I close this chapter, I am reminded of my childhood friend who I went to visit in the mental health facility. She unintentionally taught me that I need to love myself in every situation. Later in life, she and I had the opportunity to talk. At that time, she was on medication, living with her mother and her children, and taking it one day at a time. The last I heard, she was moving out of her mother's house and getting back with her husband after years of separation. I think about her often. I pray that she is well, and I wish her all of the happiness and self-love that her heart can hold. It is because I lived vicariously through her experience that I cherish myself, recognize that I am a unique gift, and love myself unconditionally each day. I listen for God's voice of love in all that I do, and I honor His love by how I treat and honor myself.

I wish you self-love! I hope you love yourself through respect, patience, restoration, and forgiveness—just because you're worth it! I must go now, because I have an appointment to keep. My cuticles need some care, and there's a massage chair at the nail salon waiting just for me!

EMBRACING THE MESSAGE

Loving Yourself for Yourself

- Love is action. Treat yourself well.

- Love is patient. Take time out for yourself.

- Love is respect. You are worthy and valuable. Don't settle for less.

- Love is forgiveness. Let it go.

Scripture Reflection

Love is patient; love is kind and envies no one. Love is never boastful, nor conceited, nor rude; never selfish, not quick to take offense. There is nothing love cannot face; there is no limit to its faith, its hope, and endurance. In a word, there are three things that last forever: faith, hope, and love; but the greatest of them all is love.

—1 Corinthians 13:4

Journal Notes: Loving Yourself for Yourself

Put on your favorite soft jam. (I like instrumental, classical, and of course, Luther Vandross's songs!) Sit quietly, and answer the questions below. Keep your answers short, simple, and real. Be in the moment. Don't edit or define your thoughts. Just respond from your heart.

1. What do you do just for yourself?

2. Do you feel guilty doing things for yourself? Why or why not?

3. What is something about you that you find hard to love? How will you lovingly embrace that part of yourself?

4. Think of a time when you disrespected yourself. Why did you treat yourself as less than what you are? What would you do differently now?

5. Who do you admire for how he or she seems to treat himself or herself? How can you emulate some of this person's traits?

6. What was the most defining message for you from this chapter?

7. How will you implement it into your life?

Remember, love just is. It does not have to be created. It is inside you, just begging to radiate from within.

CHAPTER 3

Reclaim the Power Within

There's a rap song from the '80s by the group Snap called "I've Got the Power." When the funkadelic music beat comes on, from out of nowhere, a woman's voice belts out, "I've got the power!" Well, I'm here to tell you that you've got the power! You just need to reclaim it!

Just because you don't notice something doesn't mean that it's not there and hasn't always been there, just waiting for you to acknowledge it. The average heart beats sixty to seventy times per minute, whether you notice it or not. The earth rotates around the sun regardless of your acknowledgement, and the electrical power in the wiring behind your walls is there whether or not you think about its purpose and capabilities. Still, you expect your heart to beat, morning to turn to night, and light to come on when you flip the switch.

Like flipping a switch, many times, we leave the light off in our lives and believe that because it is off, there is no power. We stumble around in the darkness, believing what we see instead of remembering what we have within. No matter where you are in life or who you are with, no matter what you have done, you have more than enough power within you to change yourself, reinvent your circumstances, and recreate what you want your life to become. But you must first remember that the power, the light, the vision, the passion, is within you. It flows throughout your being. It is there for the taking, and once you've decided to accept yourself as a beautiful person with more than everything you need to enjoy this journey, then you must claim all that belongs to you by first reclaiming what is hidden deep inside.

For some of us, this is not easy. Some of us do not believe that we have what we need to move our lives forward or pick ourselves up from where we are and start anew. Some of us believe that we are powerful and can change our circumstances, but we do not claim it and sink into self-pity and self-doubt. In both circumstances, the lack of reclaiming the power within leads to frustration, disappointment, and getting stuck.

The definition of the word *claim* is "to demand as a right; to assert as a fact; to require as due or fitting". *Reclaiming your power is taking what is already there.* Think about it. If you walk into a dry cleaner to get your clothes, you are confident that once you present the ticket, you will get your clothing. There's no doubt in your mind. Even if you don't present your ticket at some cleaners, just by giving the attendant your name, you can reclaim your clothing. You see, you are confident that your clothes are there, because you put them there to reclaim them when you were ready. It's the same with the built-in power you have inside yourself. It has been there and is waiting on you to reclaim it. It is under your name, and all you have to do is ask for it, confidently knowing that it is yours. You can reclaim it when you are ready or when it is needed the most.

This is the metaphor that I tried to explain to a teacher's aide at school. I was on my way to cafeteria duty when I saw her from afar. She usually was very pleasant, but on this day, she seemed very despondent—as if she had lost her best friend. I quickened my pace to catch up to her and ask her what was wrong. Although she denied anything was wrong, the tear stains on her cheeks gave it away. I asked her if she wanted to walk around the bus loop and talk about it, thinking that it was job-related and that there was some way that I could assist.

The aide told me a story of the night before and how her husband had belittled her about her weight. She agreed with him and attributed his meanness to his battle with alcohol. She took care of the kids, did the household chores, and was working as hard as she could to maintain her job and juggle her responsibilities. She thought she would leave this time, because she couldn't take it anymore, but what would happen to her and the kids? Her salary wasn't enough to maintain the household bills. How would she manage on her own? She told me that she needed him as she shamefully dropped her eyes.

It was difficult to listen to this giving, compassionate woman as she ignored the power she had within to change her situation. I could see that she was hurt by her husband's words and perplexed by the choices that she had to make. Should she stay or should she leave? Should she deny herself or reclaim her power? And did she have enough power to step out on her own?

The way I saw it, she was already raising the children, taking care of the household, and paying part of the expenses. He would probably have to give some type of support if she decided to leave. She and her children would probably be happier and healthier without the alcohol and verbal abuse in the home. However, she could not see this—or if she could, she did not want to accept it. More importantly and disappointingly, she could not see the power she had within herself to accept this vision for her life. She ultimately decided to stay, saying that God and her faith would see her through.

I truly believe that God—the source of all goodness—wants the best for us. I believe that He made it very clear that husbands should treat their wives the way that Jesus treated the church. Jesus loved the church, worshiped it, and ultimately laid His life down for it (Ephesians 5:25–27). There is nowhere in those lines that says that He insulted it, abused it, and made it feel worthless.

I do believe in forgiveness. I believe in second chances, depending on the circumstances. However, I also believe that if we reclaim the power within us, we will not be afraid to step out on faith. When we step out in faith, we will not doubt that the power we have inside will sustain us and see us through nor will we worry about the ultimate outcome, because we will know that it will be only for our good.

I learned this a long time ago from watching a close friend. She met a companion who put her down for no reason at all. He criticized the food she cooked, her clothes, and almost every choice that she made. He had a comment for *everything,* and his comments were never kind—always degrading and insulting. Because her parents divorced, she at first tried to make things work by overlooking the cruelty behind his words, taking what he said as constructive criticism, and finally, just ignoring him.

One day, my friend got tired. She got tired of making excuses for him, looking the other way, trying to understand, and praying the same prayer that God had already answered, yet she could not accept His response. Finally, she remembered her God-given strength and power, and as if going to the dry cleaners to get what belonged to her, she reclaimed them. When she reclaimed her power that was there, patiently waiting for her to remember, recall, and reactivate, she stood up for herself and put him in his place. His words no longer held her hostage. She found her freedom in the power she always had.

When you reclaim the power within, you acknowledge that you have all that you need to make it through your situation—whether that means garnering enough strength to stay in a situation that you work at turning around or whether you decide it's time to leave. The acknowledgment of your own inner power points you in a direction to embrace your confidence and put on your armor of self-revelation. Asserting what rightfully belongs to you, you say to yourself and the world that you can handle the situation and refuse to let the situation handle you. You no longer become a victim but a victor, because you decide to believe that you can change your circumstance to receive the goodness that you deserve.

> When you reclaim the power within, you acknowledge that you have all that you need to make it through your situation.

Before you think that I am promoting a cookie-cutter, syrupy-sweet self-help prescription, think again. I am encouraging you to dig deep back to the time when you didn't even know who you were. You were pooping in your pants and dribbling from the corner of your mouth; yet you knew instinctively that you were going to crawl. You didn't question or second-guess it. Then you knew that you were going to walk, and you either figured it out by yourself or had assistance from your parents. There was no thought to it—just a willingness to do it. Tap into that knowledge that you have everything you need to take that step, be willing and confident that you can move forward, and within time, you will. All you have to do is acknowledge the power and know that it is there for the asking—actually, for the taking—anytime, anywhere, and in any situation.

I should know. I had to remember my inner strength and reclaim it when I left my husband with my two-year-old in search of what I called a "break" from my broken marriage. I escaped to Virginia, the state where my father lived. It was supposed to be my refuge. Surprisingly, as I lay in bed in my father's house, I did not feel safe but more insecure than I had ever felt in New York. There I was—a homeowner, a parent, a grown woman who was independent and took care of everything for herself and her family. In Virginia, I was homeless, jobless, and carrying around the brokenness of my marriage in my heart.

My dad and his family tried to show support; his wife even took me to the state office to get welfare and food stamps. Oh, yes, she went there! As she said, I had to survive for me and my child. I didn't believe that I had the strength to tell her that I didn't want to go, because I didn't know who I was at the time. I felt like nothing, nobody, worthless—a complete failure who had messed up her life that had so much potential and hope.

As I drowned in my own pity party, I took an application from the unconcerned, bored woman from behind the security glass window. I sat down next to a few other women—some of whom had children running around the open bay office. As my father's wife waited, I began to fill out the application. When I got to the part that asked for my level of education, my inner voice asked me, "Melissa, what in the hell are you doing?" Here I was, Dr. Melissa Harts, filling out an application for government assistance after being in the state for less than two weeks and not sending out one job application. By being there at that time in my life, I was giving up without even trying.

I left the state office like a patient who had a sleep disorder and was given a dose of L-dopa for an awakening. I realized that I had to try, and more importantly, that I had all that I needed to change my circumstances, as dire as they may have seemed at the time. I had to reclaim my life and identity before handing them over to a system so nonchalantly, and I had to decide to reclaim the power I had within—if not for myself, then for my daughter, who depended on me. I started to job hunt, sent out applications, and within three months of my arrival, I had a part-time teaching job at a technical college and signed the lease on my new apartment.

I moved out. Yes, I packed again! I lived in the apartment—one paycheck away from being evicted. My mother, who lived in Florida, even sent boxes of food for me, because she was afraid that I did not have enough in the refrigerator. I still remember the foiled, cooked roast and frozen goods that she packed in dry ice. My dad came over and left milk and eggs in the refrigerator as well.

I tried to just take one day at a time and believe in all that I had in me to keep moving forward. But one day, the reality of my situation hit me hard. As I sat alone in the $500-a-month apartment in Nowhereland, Virginia, a blanket of emptiness engulfed me. The realization that my life was not what I had intended, my marriage was over, and I was the only link between life and death for my only child rocked me to tears. I moaned from the deepest part of my being. The sound and hollowness of it frightened me as I put my hand over my mouth, trying to force it back into the abyss from which it came.

I didn't want to awaken my two-year-old, who was sleeping soundly in my bed, but I couldn't stop this uncontrollable urge to scream and run through the darkness of the apartment in the middle of the night. As I got out of bed, I continued to tightly clutch my mouth as the sound overtook my body, and I started to gyrate uncontrollably. I collapsed to my knees in the middle of the living room, tears streaming down my face, rocking back and forth as the force from the moaning overtook me. I couldn't talk, and I gasped for breath as the lump of emotional pain traveled up my chest and lodged itself in my throat.

I couldn't articulate what I felt or why this sudden burst of emotion wrapped me into this pitiful position. I had done everything the right way. I was a dutiful wife to the husband who ignored and insulted me. I was an educated woman who was one paycheck away from being homeless in a state that was supposed to be my refuge.

All I could do was moan, sob, and moan some more. I looked up as headlights from a car beamed through the window. I stopped crying long enough to hear myself sigh. The emotional lump was still lodged in my burning throat, but in a faint whisper, I heard my spirit say, "My God, my God. Why have you abandoned me?" *A little bit dramatic,* I thought as I wiped my wet face on my nightshirt. My spirit continued to plead as I rocked myself back and forth in the darkness. No answers came. No voice boomed from heaven. No beacon of light shined from the window. But I heard the slam of a car door from the street below, a sudden chorus of dogs barking, the panting sound of my breath, and an eerie silence that filled the room.

Realizing that I was cold, I pulled myself up to the reality of the nothingness that engulfed me. I slowly walked into my bedroom and sat on the edge of the bed, staring at my expression in the mirror. I could hear my daughter breathing rhythmically in a deep sleep that I began to crave. I lay my head on the pillow, stared at the ceiling, and listened to my heartbeat fluttering quickly in my chest. Then the silence was broken by a gentle calm as I watched shadows created by the cars that passed by the window. I felt an unexpected comfort in the silence as it embraced me, and the emotional weight of the night slowly lifted. I knew that I was not alone. I knew that the miracle sleeping next to me was proof of that. And I knew somewhere deep in me that it would be all right. I didn't know how, but I felt that surely, it would all work out … somehow.

I rolled to the side, where my daughter slept angelically, and begged sleep to come so that I did not have to think about my life anymore. But instead of sleep came a silent prayer to God that came from deep within my subconscious mind. It was buried behind all of the anger, disappointment, and frustration. I asked the Lord to get me out of Virginia and help me find a better job other than the one I had. I asked Him to help me heal, move forward, and not let the past steal my blessings for the future.

I'd like to say that God came in a puff of light or that a booming voice shook the room, but none of that took place. This time, the calm turned to agitation and a strong desire to get up and listen to music. I got out of bed, accepted the fact that I would get no rest that night, and I put on a Yolanda Adams CD. I had listened to her before but never really paid attention to the words in her songs. But that night was different, and when she belted out, "The battle is not yours. It's the Lord's" (2 Chronicles 20:15). I felt that God had answered my prayers.

I jumped to my feet and sang the song a little too loudly, waking Katieri right out of her sleep. After hushing her back to sleep, I called my mother, and without a penny to my name or a clue as to what I was going to do, I told her, "Mommy, find me a house in Florida." I knew that I had to leave and that there was something better for me. I didn't want to live this way, and something deep within me told me that I did not have to, because I created this situation, and I had the power to change it.

The house didn't come right away, but the job did. I had applied a few weeks before to be a substitute teacher for the public school system. I was told that because of the timing of year (December), I might not get a long-term substitute position, but they would call me if daily substituting came up. Without a steady income, I would be stuck in Virginia—and stuck in the emotional corner that I put myself in. When the phone call came in from the principal of a local high school for a long-term substitute position teaching English, I grabbed it like the lifeline that it was. After getting the job, I sent out applications to every school in the county in Florida where my mother lived. I heard back from two. After applying and interviewing, I was offered both.

Although I retell my story as if everything happened automatically, it did not. But I trusted that God was going to work it out for me somehow. I had a deep knowledge that everything would be all right.

In the meantime, I wrote a three-column list every night. The first column was labeled "What Do I Want" and included moving to my own house in Florida, getting a job to support my daughter and myself, and peace of mind. The second was labeled "What Do I Have" and included all of the things I was grateful for at the time. Then in the third column, I listed "What I Know For Sure." There, I wrote, "I know for sure that I have everything that I need to survive. I know that God is going to help me through. I know that I must leave to find my peace." I didn't know how things would end up, but I planted seeds and hoped that the rain would fall so that they would blossom into something beautiful and divine.

After choosing one of the two teaching offers, I longed to hear from the realtor that my loan application was approved despite my low credit score and no money to put down. Well, the seeds I planted and prayed over were watered. The house loan came through, and I packed again. This time, I headed for a better life in Florida. However, I found out from the realtor that he had to send the application to seven separate lenders before one finally agreed to give me the loan for my house.

Seven different lenders denied me before one said yes, but I kept believing that I deserved better. Just as I packed each box one at a time in New York, as I packed the boxes in Virginia, I knew that my daughter and I deserved more. I knew that I had enough on the inside of me to change the situation in which I had put myself. And I knew that God did not make me feeble, defeated, and worthless.

I believe what Paul said to the Romans: "In all these things, we are more than conquerors through him that loved us" (Romans 8:37). I say the same thing to you. You are more than a conqueror. Reclaim your power. If you have denied it, lied to yourself and said that you don't have it, or given it away to someone else, then stop! Know that you have the power in you to progress, change wrong to right, rectify a situation, and make it better—not because I tell you so, but because it is so!

Don't let what the news reports tell you about the economy infect your mind and force you to believe that your power is not there! Don't let the fact that you are not getting responses to the job applications you sent out steal the hope that you will get a position where you can make a difference and make the salary that you need, want, and deserve! Don't let talking heads on television tell you that you can't make it in this day and age; this is an insult to the power you have within to change your perception and ultimately alter your reality.

> **Redirect your thoughts, reactivate your creativity, and reclaim your right to have what you deserve!**

There is nothing so hard in this life that you cannot get through. Others have done it successfully, so why not you? Redirect your thoughts, reactivate your creativity, and reclaim your right to have what you deserve! You have the power within you to create a better reality, change your life from going in one direction, redesign your goals, and reconstruct your dreams. Go back to what you know and who you are, reclaim these things, and fix your situation! I did, and so can you!

If you think I'm crazy—and as the older folks would say, "done lost her mind"—think again. I told this to my brother, who was in a no-win situation at work, and he is now in a new job. He makes a higher salary and is happier with his career than he has ever been. He reclaimed his power and changed his life in three weeks. My heart hurt every time he called me from New York to tell me about the drama at work. There, he was demoted because of an insecure supervisor who was intimidated by anyone smarter, younger, and upwardly mobile. This jealous supervisor did everything she could to keep others down, looked for them to slip up rather than trying to help them up when they fell, and found the *I* in the word *team,* even though no one else saw it.

My brother was at his wit's end, forced to work weekends and deal with issues on his day off, just because he wanted to keep his job and pay his bills. He got calls from the office on his day off and was expected to come in and resolve the situation. I told him, "Preston, send your resume out. You have a lot to offer, but not at this company." He gave me all the reasons why he couldn't and shouldn't send out his resume. He said the company where he worked had great benefits and was a large known company in the field, jobs were hard to find, and, of course, the economy was bad.

I told my brother that he owed it to himself to first decide to leave. Once he did that, he needed to reclaim his power and believe that he could find a job somewhere else and be appreciated for all that he had to offer. Between me preaching to him and him being afraid that he would lose his job, he sent out six resumes. The last one that he faxed was for a job that he wanted. Within minutes of sending his resume through the fax, a secretary from the company contacted him and set up an interview.

My brother was interviewed, and within a week (actually, the day before Thanksgiving), the director wanted to meet him. He was hired after Christmas. The company gave him a raise, weekends off, and the peace and recognition that he deserved. An article was written in an industry newsletter about him. The executive director praised him for the work he had done after a month on the job. But most importantly, the joy in his voice confirmed that he had reclaimed the power that he always had within to make a difference in his own life.

If I am crazy, then so is he—and you can be, too. Be daring enough to tap into what already exists inside of you. Whether you are trying to change jobs, change a relationship, or change your style, you have the power to make it happen. Don't believe that you can't do what you set your mind to do. It may take a few steps, and it may take longer than you may want, but it will happen because of the innate power you have within. Wayne Dwyer says it best in his inspirational book *The Power of Intention:* "Your goal is to eliminate any distance between what you desire and that from which you pull into your life. Abundance and success aren't out there waiting to show up for you. You are already it, and the Source can only provide you with what it is, and consequently, what you are already."[5]

The power you have within you is the same power others

---

5   Wayne Dyer, *The Power of Intention* (Carlsbad, CA: Hay House, Inc., 2004), 183.

have within them. I saw a picture of Grammy Award-winning recording artist Mary J. Blige. She had a T-shirt that read, "I'm Power." Mary J. Blige came up from the streets of Brooklyn, New York (not too far from Queens, where I grew up), did not graduate from high school, dealt with difficult relationships, and struggled as an aspiring rap artist. She is now a multimillionaire with her own company, happily married, and involved in various community organizations to inspire young people and women to believe in their own power to change and make a difference.

Mary J. Blige's T-shirt reminded me of the biblical story of Moses at the burning bush. God sent Moses to Pharaoh to tell him, "Let my people go." I imagine Moses thinking, *Who am I to ask the great Pharaoh to let the Israelites go?* However, what he said instead was, "Who should I tell him is sending me?" God answered with what I believe to be the most powerful words in the Bible: "I AM that I AM" (Exodus 3:14).

Wayne Dwyer calls this "I Am" the source of goodness, where purpose and intention meet. He refers to this "I Am" as the Spirit. I call him God. Whatever you call Him, this source of goodness is all-powerful and the originator of creation. If we are from the source of goodness that is powerful, then why are we not powerful? Why do we believe that we do not have any power? Why should we hold our heads down and feel powerless? We, like Mary J., should, wear T-shirts every day that say, "I'm Power." We should remember that we come from the great I Am and know that we are divinely *enough* as we are and in our very creation.

I imagine that when Moses, dressed in sandals and holding a wooden staff, told Pharaoh that I Am sent him. Pharaoh must have thought quizzically, "Who sent you? So, *you are* the person who I Am sent?" Of course, as the Bible tells us, Pharaoh thought Moses was a joke and refused to let the Israelites go. As the story goes, ten plagues came. Then the Israelites left after I Am parted the sea for them while drowning Pharaoh's men (Exodus 12:37–15:21). I imagine that Pharaoh went back to Egypt, sat on his now empty throne, marveled at the power of I Am, and wished he had done things differently.

If we are from I Am, then we believe that we are powerful, able, capable, abundant, and all that we need. I Am sent you into this world so that you are powerful, able, capable, abundant, and all that you need. You have the power within you to receive all of the goodness and blessings this life has to offer. Don't forget that! Reclaim it! Reactivate it! Renew it! It's in you just because of the fact that *you are*.

Even though you may not own an "I'm Power" T-shirt, act as if you do. You are already wired with power. It is electrifying. It is inside you, whether you acknowledge it or not. It beats through your soul every second of the day, radiates within, and is part of your very essence. Put a smile on your face, look at your situation, and belt out from the pit of your being, "I've got the power!"

EMBRACING THE MESSAGE

Reclaiming the Power Within

🕊 *Reclaim* who you are. Don't believe what news reports and other people tell you about what you can or cannot do about a situation that affects your life.

🕊 *Reclaim* your belief in what you can do. Think out of the box about how to solve or better your situation. Make a plan, and listen within for ways to tweak it.

🕊 *Reclaim* what you know is true. Know that your power is there. Just as you know your name, know that you have the power to redesign and redirect your life.

Scripture Reflection

I AM that I AM.

—Exodus 3:4

Journal Notes: Reclaiming the Power Within

Some songs just get you fired up—the ones that have you dancing around the house like you've lost your mind. Blast one of those songs. It's okay if your family thinks you're crazy. Feel powerful. Embrace the moment. Then as you catch your breath, answer the questions below.

1. When was the last time that you felt powerful?

2. Describe that feeling.

3. What does the word *powerful* mean to you?

4. How can you feel powerful daily? What choices do you have to make? What things in your life do you need to change?

5. What do you know to be true about your life? How have you come to those conclusions?

6. Listen to yourself for five minutes. What are your worries? What are your hopes? How do you move forward to reclaim what you truly deserve?

7. What was the most defining message for you from this chapter?

8. How will you implement it into your life?

Remember, power is knowledge that you come from a divine being and that you came here equipped with all you need for this journey.

ᒡᔅ CHAPTER 4 ᔇᔊ

Unlimit Your Limitations

"I can't."

I can't tell you how many times I have said those two words out loud to myself or to someone or internally. I should know better, because every time I try, I succeed. Why are those two words so easy to say and so readily adopted as part of my vocabulary? It seems that it would be just as easy to say "I can." But "I can't" gives us an excuse. It gives us a comfortable place where we can hide and not explain or explore the possibilities of being able to do something spectacular or seemingly extraordinary.

My father reminds me every so often of a playground accident that I had when I was a child. I was about five when I walked up the steps of the sliding board, as I had done on several occasions before. This time, though, my dad was taking pictures of me to capture this moment in a plastic-covered photo album. I looked at him below. I somehow missed my step and fell to the black rubber mat that not only cushioned my fall, but also probably saved my life. My dad comforted me and told me to "Get back up, and try again."

I'm not sure what I said, but I had no intention of getting back up on that sliding board that looked fifty feet high from where I was curled up on the ground. I know that I said, "I can't."

My dad, in his prescience, said, "You must, because if you don't, you will always be afraid of the sliding board." I got up with much encouragement from my dad and a heart filled with trepidation and worry. I clung to the iron railing and concentrated on my grip as I willed my feet to step on each stair. I did not turn around for fear that I would end up where I began—on the rubber mat waiting menacingly below. When I finally sat on the top stair with my legs hanging over the edge of the slide, I remember how excited I was, looking at my dad cheering me on below. The fear was replaced with the expectation of the joy that was about to come.

As the sun reflected on the shiny aluminum, I let go and put my hands up with a loud *"Wee."* I slid into my dad's arms, welcoming me at the end of my three-second adventure. That day, I must have worn out my pant bottom going down that slide! The lesson that day is one that I often forget: unlimit your limitations. Turn your impossibilities into possibilities by saying and believing, "I can."

My dad had it right when he told me to get back up on that slide, because had I not, I would have been paralyzed by an unexplainable fear that could have taken root into other areas of my life. If I had not gotten back on the sliding board, I would not have had the joy of swooshing down, carefree, into my father's arms. I also would not have the memory of all the other joyful experiences in playgrounds and parks going up and down the slide.

I sometimes reflect on the sliding board experience I had as a child, because it seems very simple. You've heard it before: *get up, dust yourself off, and try again.* But sometimes, life just keeps knocking us down, and it gets harder and harder to get up and want to try again.

A dear friend of mine has wanted to be superintendent for many years. We both work in the same building. She has worked very hard and is extremely qualified to be superintendent. However, the position always eludes her for reasons beyond her control. The first time she applied for the position, her application (along with others) was rejected because of information needed that was not listed on the original job posting. The second time she applied, she was only allowed to be an interim superintendent through a narrow vote. The third time she applied, she did not get the job and was told that it was because of her limited experience. When I spoke to her, she seemed tired of the process, but she wasn't broken. She told me that she would continue to apply, because she believed that it was her divine destiny to be a superintendent.

> **Turn your impossibilities into possibilities by saying and believing, "I can."**

My friend kept getting up on the slide, although each time was harder and harder. She did not limit herself to what others thought of her. She kept her focus, because she believed that she deserved the position. There were no excuses or limiting thoughts—only the desire to continue to move forward toward the promise she felt she deserved.

I share her story, because although it oozes with positive thinking and "believe in yourself" mantras, I did not internalize it that way. I took her "I can" to be my "I can't." In watching all that she encountered the three times she applied for the same position that she truly wanted, I withdrew to my safety zone of "I can't." After all, I had an example before me of why I couldn't. *I can't be promoted, because she wasn't, even though she tried. I can't get promoted, because there are limited high-level positions here. I can't get promoted, because I'm not qualified enough. I can't get promoted because of the downturn in the economy, and there are no other jobs anywhere else.*

Because the words *I can't* are so comforting, we rely on them to take the pressure off of us to do something different. The words *I can't* put a period where a question mark should be. The statement is definitive and answers the question "Why not?" all the time—especially when it is partnered with the word *because.*

In his book *Excuses Begone,* Wayne Dwyer talks about the limitations we put on ourselves when we believe the excuses that we give ourselves. Instead of making excuses, he encourages readers to find the possibilities in every situation and follow the path of reprogramming our inner language to make a difference in our lives. If I rule out all of my excuses, then I'm left with the question that we are all born with: Why not? That simple question opens the door to all other possibility questions, such as *Why shouldn't I apply? What are the possibilities available to me if I do get the job? What rewards and benefits will I receive? What will I be able to do then that I am unable to do now?*

The questions that stem from "Why not" put us on the road of possibilities. They encourage us to explore what we have within us that can make what seems impossible happen. When we rule out the limiting beliefs and the *I can't* thoughts, then we put ourselves in a position to receive all that our hearts can hold. I know this is true, because after watching my friend constantly not get the promotion, I believed that I could not be promoted either. I compared myself to her and thought, *If she can't, then what makes me think that I can?* How rational is that?

I limited myself based on my perception of someone else's experience. When I realized how ridiculous this was, I thought, *Why can't I get promoted?* The only person limiting me was me. I applied for a job in another county at which I would make more money than I made in the position I held. I made it to the superintendent-level interview, and I was relaxed, confident, and at peace. I ended the interview with a statement of gratitude.

I didn't get the job. But the reward to believing that I could was that I was asked to apply for another job more in line with my current experience. I was the only one who interviewed for the job. I don't know if I got it, but it was mostly about the process of releasing my limitations. I was grateful that I went through the process, because what I learned was invaluable to my individual and professional growth. I learned that I do not need to limit my possibilities, because as long as I believe in what is within me, I will always achieve great rewards, including raises, new friends, more confidence, and increased knowledge.

Ralph Waldo Emerson said it best in the nineteenth century when he said, "What lies behind us and what lies before us are tiny matters compared to what lies within us." What you say to yourself on the inside is reflected on the outside. Your internal thoughts and beliefs free you from limitations so that you can reap your rewards.

What Lies Within Us

Don't get what I'm saying confused with the old adage "Believe it, and you will achieve it." You can believe something all you want and still not achieve it. But if you believe in something, do it, and work at it, you will achieve greater success than you ever thought possible. That's not as neat as the old adage, but it's what needs to be done. Just changing your attitude is not enough if the change is not followed by consistent and persistent action.

> **Your internal thoughts and beliefs free you from limitations so that you can reap your rewards.**

I'm reminded of a former student, John (name changed for anonymity), who was told and believed that he could not succeed. He came from a difficult background. His mother had multiple children and was apparently on drugs. She sent John to live with his paternal grandmother, who loved him dearly but couldn't make up for the rejection that he felt from an early age. His father was not in his life, and John struggled in every subject area in school. He had a temper, and most of his teachers did not want to work with him. When he arrived in my sixth-grade class, John was conditioned to believe that he could not succeed. He had seen much failure—not only in his own life, but also in his parents' lives. His former teachers labeled him as non-academic and wanted him tested for behavioral issues.

In my class, John was quiet. He did his work when he was held accountable. If he thought that you would let him get by with the labels that he came to believe about himself, then he did not do his work. When he responded to questions, he was bright and articulate. He had beautiful handwriting but needed direction with grammar and syntax. When he did not perform well on a test, I questioned whether he studied. He told me he hadn't, because he stayed up late watching television. He then said, "Why should I study when I can't get a good grade anyway?"

Buried in John's being were the simple destructive words, "I can't." "I can't study" meant *I can't do well in school. I can't achieve my goals. I can't succeed.* John, his grandmother, and I came up with a plan to help him succeed. It started with him taking one step at a time up the sliding board and not looking back. Though he was scared and doubted that he may make it to the top, he had to press forward with our encouragement and support. I'm proud to say that he made it to the eighth grade. He eventually went on to high school, and I hope he will go on to college. Sometimes I wonder where he would be had he not stopped saying, "I can't." I wonder what statistical category he would have fallen into: jobless, homeless, incarcerated, addicted, or deceased.

This may seem harsh, but it's real. When we limit ourselves, we limit all of the positive outcomes that can become part of our lives. When we say, "I can't have someone who loves me," we put a hold on all the people who can love us. When we say, "I can't get that job," we limit the resources that we have at our disposal and the possibility of financial increase, professional growth, and personal development that could occur. When we say, "I can't have that house," we dismiss the ability that we have to live and maintain a certain lifestyle. When we say, "I can't do this or that," we deny our divine right to be able to do something. Putting limitations on who we are, what we are capable of having, and what we are able to do interferes with our divine destiny to be abundantly joyful and happy.

My student, John, had to consistently turn off the television and study. In order to achieve his academic goals, he had to do more than just believe. Once he believed that he could get better grades, he had to practice, study, turn in assignments on time, and pay attention in class. To tap into his limitless possibilities, he had to work hard at what he wanted to achieve. I'm sure he was afraid, but he stuck to his newfound belief in his possibilities and worked hard in each class until he made it to high school.

You, too, must move beyond the cliché "I can't." Begin affirming that you *can,* whether you believe it at first or not. Will yourself to say that you can move beyond your current circumstance, have better, receive more, and deserve to be more. Don't accept any less than what you truly deserve to have and be, which are greater than whatever you imagine for yourself.

Michael Jordan is best known for being one of the best defensive players in basketball, winning six NBA championships, and receiving five NBA Most Valuable Team Player awards, just to name a few of his achievements. Some may not know that he started out at Emsley A. Laney High School in Wilmington, North Carolina, where he played baseball, football, and basketball. During his sophomore year, he tried out for varsity basketball but did not make the team, because he was too short at five foot eleven! But Michael was determined to prove that he could be a contender on the court, and he tried out again the next summer.

In 1981, Jordan received a basketball scholarship to the University of North Carolina at Chapel Hill. The NBA drafted him three years later, and the rest is history. I wonder what would have happened if Michael Jordan gave up after not making his high school team. I wonder how many hours he practiced to stay on top of his game to receive a scholarship to the University of North Carolina at Chapel Hill. He worked hard, and he did not limit himself due to fear or the possibility of failure. He says it best on a poster showing him making his trademark "Air Jordan" jump shot: "I've missed more than nine thousand shots in my career. I've lost almost three hundred games. Twenty-six times, I've been trusted to take the game winning shot and missed. I've failed over and over and over again in my life … and that is why I have succeeded."

Stop limiting yourself. Stop holding on to impossibility and making excuses for why you should not do something you know that you want to do. Stop preventing yourself from reaching out to meet your destiny—the one that was ingrained in you before you were even born.

Tap into Your Talents

The people we consider successful—either in our communities or in the media—do not limit themselves, because they know they were born with gifts and talents. When you believe that you have something to offer, you will do what you can to express it and open yourself up to possibilities. I struggle with this all of the time. I have to remind myself and convince myself to do things that I have ingrained in my head that I can't.

At a recent board meeting, I was on the agenda to present awards to my staff. I requested to be on the agenda, because I wanted my staff to be recognized for their huge accomplishments. However, I tormented myself that entire day about what I would say. I told myself, "I *can't* do this, because I hate to speak in front of people." This lasted up until the time the board meeting began, and I had to stop myself and say, "Girl, this is an opportunity to showcase their accomplishments. You are divinely capable of speaking articulately. After all, you've done it before." I took a deep breath and reminded myself of what I knew to be true. When I was called to the podium, I had a comfortable exchange with the superintendent. The mood was joyful, and everything went well.

I learned that I need to be comfortable in my divine talents and know that they can only accomplish something good if I do not limit myself and negatively impact my experience by thinking the wrong thoughts. I am moved by the parable of the talents (Matthew 25:15–30). Three men were given a certain amount of silver, or talents. Before the master went away, he gave one five talents, another two talents, and the last one talent. The first two invested theirs and doubled them, while the last guy buried his, because he was afraid to lose it. When the master came back, he was pleased with the first two, because they doubled their investments. He called them good and faithful servants. But he was displeased with the last one, calling him wicked and slothful. The master banished the last servant and gave his one talent away.

When I first read the story as a child, I thought the last servant was smart! He took what he had and kept it. He was safe. At least he did not take a risk and lose what was given to him. He held what his master gave him in great care. However, as an adult, I realize he was foolish, because he let his fear limit his possibilities. He did not believe in himself enough to double what he was given. He did not share his talent with others, and he did not try to improve on what he was given. He was guilty as charged.

I don't want to be like him. I don't want to hide my talents and then at the end of my life have nothing to show, because I buried them. I want to exhaust all I have within me. Joel Osteen, the pastor of Lakewood Church in Houston, Texas, has said several times that the richest place on earth is in the graveyard, where there are many buried talents. Those people, like the wicked, slothful servant in the parable, hid their talents until it was too late. I don't want that to be me! I know that you don't want that to be you!

I hope you understand why God would be disappointed in us if we buried our talents and limited all that He gave us from the beginning of time. I would be disappointed in my child if I gave her something to use, and she let it sit there to rot.

I have put money aside for my daughter to go to college. Her four years of tuition will be paid, should she choose to go. I believe in her, because she is academically talented, and I know that she will do well in college and beyond. Let's say I go away the year before she goes to college and tell her that her college is paid for; all she has to do is apply and get accepted. Imagine that I come back two years later, fully expecting her to be in her first year of college, because she had no limitations. She's smart, organized, goal-oriented, and can go to college tuition-free. If she is not enrolled in college, I would be livid—just like the master in the parable of talents. I believed in her abilities enough to invest in her. I believed in her talents and worked hard to give her the opportunity to use them. All she had to do was go.

You are more than able to do what you have been called to

do. Some have the ability to sing, dance, lead, draw, be flexible, etc. But we all have an obligation to use the divine talents that we are given. We don't have the luxury of limiting ourselves and telling ourselves that we can't do something when we are wired with abilities. We always have something to do and are more than able to do it—or at least try. We must tap into our talents and not limit our own abilities. We shouldn't compare ourselves to others but do what we can do and do it well. It is our obligation while we are on this journey. It is part of our mission. It is part of who we are and what we are called to do.

> We all have an obligation to use the divine talents that we are given.

Don't deny it or hide it by cutting yourself off from the blessings that belong to you. You are meant to excel. You are meant to enjoy abundance. You are meant to shine. Tap into all that you are, and accept it as who you are called to be. Most importantly, remember that you are the light of the world. "A city that is set on a hill cannot be hid. Neither do men light a candle, and put it under a bushel, but on a candlestick, and it gives light to all that are in the house. Let your light so shine before men, that they may see your good works, and glorify your Father which is in heaven" (Matthew 5:14–16). I didn't say it; Jesus did.

Changing Your Inner Conversations

Whatever you say to yourself, you enact. It's as if you're writing your own script, and you are starring in the play. If you tell yourself that you can't, then you won't. You create a script for yourself that you run in your mind, and it becomes your reality. Jean Piaget's schema theory[6] states that we develop categories of knowledge to help us understand our world. We process information based on our unique experiences, and we create mental categories that dictate our interpretation.

Let's take my sliding board experience as an example. If I had not gone back up on the sliding board, then my schema for sliding boards would be dangerous, painful, and fearful. I would develop a mental category, and every time I saw a sliding board, the associated images would be verified through my negative experience. But because I went back up on the slide and had a different experience, I changed my schema of sliding boards to *fun, adventurous,* and *welcoming.* This is Piaget's process of assimilation, which means that I used new information to change my mental image of sliding boards. To change my previous image of sliding boards, I had to have an inner conversation with myself as I walked up the steps. Yes, my father was encouraging me, but I had to will myself to go up the steps, believing that what he said was true.

Our mental pictures and categories (schemas) can limit us from doing all that we are called to do. In order to change these images, we have to create different experiences by having inner conversations with ourselves and encouraging ourselves to move beyond the words "I can't." Any conversation that you have with yourself will be manifested. I have seen it in my students who don't think they are smart enough to pass. Lo and behold, they don't pass. I've seen it in my girlfriends who say they are not

6   Jean Piaget. (1964). Part I: *Cognitive development in children: Piaget development and learning. Journal of Research in Science Teaching,* 2(3), 176-186. http://onlinelibrary.wiley.com/doi/10.1002/tea.3660020306/abstract

beautiful. Well, guess what. They are beautiful, but they slump their shoulders, wear baggy clothes, and don't act as they look.

What do you tell yourself? What images do you hold about yourself that need to be changed, reversed, or just erased altogether? When you identify those limiting thoughts and beliefs, then you can begin to work on changing them. You change them by reexamining why you feel that way about yourself or your abilities, and you have a heart-to-heart talk with yourself about your divinity.

I didn't think that I could write this book. As a matter of fact, this book was in my head five years ago. I wrote it down as one of my goals and had a plan for how I was going to accomplish writing it. I never did. I never turned on the computer or even wrote it out on a piece of paper. I was acting out the script I had in my head. I was the leading lady who walked around saying, "I can't write a book because who would read it? I can't write a book, because it will take so long. I can't write a book, because I never did before, and I don't know how." I rehearsed my lines so well that the book never got written. I even signed an internal contract with myself that included all of the reasons why the book should be written but wouldn't!

Then two years ago, I asked myself why I couldn't write the book. I was more than capable, and I believed that it was part of what I was supposed to do. The Holy Spirit would not let me rest until the book was written. I had ignored my divine instinct for so long that I felt an annoying drive to write the book. It had to be born. It had to be written to show others that they are more than enough. The more I thought about writing it, the more conversations I had with myself that changed my image of writing this book.

I talked to myself about all of the women who the book could help. I thought about how I wanted to lay out each chapter. I made lists of people who could help me. I thought about how devastating it would be if I did not follow my inner call to offer hope and show women that they have all that it takes to make it in any circumstance they may find themselves. I wanted women to believe in themselves and say, "I can make it. I am worthy, and I have every gift I need to be a blessing to those around me." "I can't" cannot exist in those thoughts. When I changed my conversation with myself, I changed my thoughts and possibilities. Now I can give freely and receive that much more.

Say, "I Can, and I Must"

This chapter was one of the hardest ones for me to write, because I constantly catch myself limiting my potential and possibilities. My excuses, negative self-talk, and irrational fears all ball up into two simple yet destructive words: *I can't.* Those words have robbed me of so many joyous moments and experiences that I should know better by now. Every time I release myself from their death grip, I am able to receive every blessing I am entitled to have.

I have enjoyed writing this chapter, because it has helped me to reflect on all of the impossibility thinking that I still hold on to. I have conjured up all of the lies that I have told myself and allowed myself to believe. I'm not going to recount them, because I have used the delete key in my mind and erased them from my inner conversations. I may still struggle with others, but I'm committed to move beyond them, tap into my talents, believe my truth, and unlock the door to the abundant life that awaits me. I hope you do the same!

I hope you move beyond the limitations and change your language to "I can, and I must." You must, because you are more than able to; you must, because you are called to bless this world with your time and talents. You must, because if you don't, you will block yourself from all that life has stored up for you to enjoy and behold.

EMBRACING THE MESSAGE

Unlimit Your Limitations

🐦 Say affirmative words to yourself: "I can. I must. I will."

🐦 The inner conversation that you have with yourself will direct how you view your possibilities.

🐦 Recreate the images you have of not being able to do something, and transform them into images of promise and ability.

🐦 Tap into your talents. Know that you came to this planet to do something special if only you will allow yourself to do it.

Scripture Reflection

Let your light so shine before men, that they may see your good works, and glorify your Father which is in heaven.

—Matthew 5:14–16

Journal Notes: Unlimit Your Limitations

Look at the sky for a few minutes. Think about how spacious it is. There are no boundaries or limits. Hold on to this feeling, and then answer the questions below.

1. What would you do if you allowed yourself the opportunity?

2. What are your goals?

3. What goals have you buried and told yourself that you can't accomplish?

4. What holds you back from trying to accomplish your goals?

5. What messages do you tell yourself daily?

6. What things do you tell yourself that you can't do? Why do you think you can't do them?

7. How can you change your inner conversation with yourself so that you are always looking at the possibilities?

8. What was the most defining message for you in this chapter?

9. How will you implement it in your life?

Remember, we were all called here to do something. Do it, and don't put limits on your possibilities.

CHAPTER 5

Embrace Your Beauty

Aromas of basil, rosemary, and onion swirled throughout the café as we stood in the long line that blocked the entrance. The enchanting combination of seafood smells from crab bisque mixed with the tantalizing scent of cheddar from something alfredo captured my senses and provoked my impatient stomach to growl. To take my mind off the impending wait for delectable ecstasy, I looked around the inviting flower shop that was adjacent to the café and to the left of the hallway near the restrooms. In the display was a brilliant red rose floating in a fishbowl of water.

As if in a hypnotic trance, I left my lunch party in the line. I was drawn to the call of this flower. The rose petals were open and inviting—each perfect in form. In its center, the unfolded petals hugged each other gently, not ready to reveal their magnificence. In its simplest form, the flower was just a clipped rose in a glass bowl, but on this day, I recognized it for what it was intended to be. It was an object of beauty. It was created to be perfect and flawless in its color, shape, and makeup. It did not question its beauty or have doubts about what it was created to be. It was a beautiful rose made to participate in the cycle of life and exist in its most perfect form. I bought the rose and kept it for a while on my bathroom counter as a reminder to enjoy beauty and remember that the same God who created the rose also created me.

It's a humbling experience to look at a rose or something in nature and marvel at its beauty. We do not question why it is beautiful. It just is. Why do we question our own beauty and magnificence? Why is it so hard for some of us to look at ourselves in the mirror and know that we are as beautiful and perfect as a rose? This is difficult for us because of the meaning that we give to beauty that is either self-prescribed or inflicted by society. I also believe that we have difficulty with our image of beauty, because we sometimes have a hard time accepting ourselves and embracing our inner divinity.

A peacock stands tall and proud and fans his tail of colorful feathers just because he can. A lion struts his stuff across the savanna with his regal head held high just because he feels like it. A male hippopotamus opens his mouth and displays his teeth when he looks to attract a female hippo. They all have an innate sense that they are beautiful and are proud to show it in their own unique ways and habitats.

Why do we hold our heads down and shy away from believing that we are divinely made and thus more beautiful than any other creature on the planet? We are told that we are made in the image of God (Genesis 1:26). God is a lot of things (this is meant reverently), but the one description that I love the most is that He is beautiful! King David said that the thing he wanted above anything that he had—including wives, gold, servants, and a mansion—was to live in the house of God all of the days of his life, look upon the beauty of the Lord, and inquire in His temple (Psalm 27:4).

The transitive property in geometry that is used to prove a theorem is this: if $A = B$ and $B = C$, then $A = C$. If God made us in His own image and God is beautiful, then we are beautiful! How can we not be? Parents know this. When children are born who came directly from their mothers and fathers, those parents know that their children are beautiful. There are no doubts in their minds. When parents look at their children, they see their children's beauty and are humbled by it. Parents take pictures of their children, show them to everyone they know, and send announcements of their birth with pictures attached via e-mail or on Facebook. Parents are tickled and want the world to see the beauty and miracle that they see.

In Isaiah 49:15–16, God reminds us that He thinks we are beautiful, too! He asks, "Can a mother forget the baby at her breast and have no compassion on the child she has borne? Though she may forget, I will not forget you! See, I have engraved you on the palms of my hands; your walls are ever before me." Wow! I love knowing that not only am I loved by the King of the universe who has not forgotten me, but He also has an image of me in the palm of His hand! Think about that! You and I *have* to be beautiful! God would not put an ugly picture on His hand.

I like to think that God shows the picture of me to the entire universe, just as I show pictures of my daughter to everyone I know. If you're like me, you have a picture of your child, grandchild, or someone you think is extraordinary somewhere on your person. I love showing pictures of my daughter, because she's beautiful! It doesn't matter what anyone thinks. I'm so proud to show off her picture. When I take her photo out of my wallet, pride wells up within me. A rush of excitement fills me in anticipation of the person seeing my child. I take out her photo as if to say, "*Ta-da!* Look how magnificent she is!" That's how we should feel about ourselves. We should remember that if the all-powerful God thinks we're beautiful enough to keep an image of us in the palm of His hand—if He made us in His own image—then we should have no doubt about our own beauty. We should walk into rooms with our heads held as if saying to the world, "*Ta-da!* Look how magnificent I am!"

The Meaning of Beauty

There are situations and experiences that make us feel ugly and unattractive. People may call us ugly or categorize us as unappealing. We may even believe that about ourselves, but that does not (and will not) make it true. I love the lyrics from Christina Aguilara's song "I Am Beautiful." It says, "I am beautiful no matter what they say. Words can't bring me down." Those words are not only the words that others say, but also the words that we tell ourselves.

If you call yourself dumb and stupid, you not only deny your own divinity, but also reject the beauty of you. If you call yourself wonderfully made, then you acknowledge your oneness with all of creation

> We should walk into rooms with our heads held as if saying to the world, "*Ta-da!* Look how magnificent I am!"

and embrace the beauty of you. If you tell yourself you are beautiful and believe that you are, then you can also spread your colorful tail feathers and walk proud like a peacock. You will saunter like the regal lion, and I'm not sure if you want to bare your teeth like the hippo, but why not? Beauty is a mindset that we must embrace if we want to fully accept ourselves.

We all have images, definitions, and stereotypes about what is beautiful and what is not. But beauty is not limited by those defining barriers. It just is beauty. As the rose that sits on my bathroom counter, it doesn't change because of my definition or your definition. It just sits elegantly in the bowl, inviting me to look at it every morning as I wash my face and stare at myself in the mirror. It reminds me that beauty is more than my limitations. It is a feeling, an existence, a state of mind. It's not superficial, vain, or pretentious. It's true and real. It exists in any situation and survives any challenge.

In the classic Disney film *Snow White and the Seven Dwarfs,* the wicked stepmother is obsessed with her own beauty. She has a magic mirror that she religiously asks the same question every day: "Mirror, mirror on the wall, who is the fairest of them all?" The mirror habitually says she is the most beautiful, of course, until one day, the script changes, and the mirror announces that Snow White has knocked the queen down to second place. It's the stepmother-stepdaughter beauty pageant with a twist. The judge is the magical mirror. Snow White's beauty is more than external, however. She has internal beauty, as she is kind to animals and old dwarf men. She sings, cleans, cooks, and can hold a decent conversation. She is not one-dimensional, like her stepmother, who is only concerned with her outward appearance.

The thing I love about this classic is that Snow White never dwells on her beauty. It is just a part of who she is. The stepmother is so jealous about it that she wants Snow White dead. The hunter is so overwhelmed by it that he can't kill her and lets her escape. The dwarfs are enamored by it as they watch her sleep in their bed that they allow her to stay in. And the prince is so entranced by it that he kisses her in her deep sleep, and they live happily ever after. Throughout the movie, though, Snow White never looks in a mirror. She doesn't talk about her beauty. The meaning that others ascribe to it does not move her in the least. She continues to be Snow White regardless of what they think or say.

Beauty, then, is deep, meaningful, captivating, and inviting! When you accept yourself and embrace the gift that you are, beauty can only radiate through. I'm not selling some facial product to you. I know from firsthand experience, because like many of you, I worried about my beauty! Most young girls do. We all want to be princesses and be pleasing to the eye. As little girls, we play dolls, dress-up, and long to be the Snow White in every movie. I can't tell you how many times I've watched *Enchanted* with my daughter, imagining that I am Jezel, being swept off my feet in the ballroom by Robert. I have pressed rewind to re-watch the scene when Prince Edward proposes to Danielle in *Ever After*. I tear up at the end of every film where the beauty gets her prince. We long to be wanted, appealing, and beautiful; when we feel that we are not, it destroys everything that God created us to be.

The meaning of beauty, then, is quite simple. It is good. As stated in chapter one, the book of Genesis tells us that when God formed the sky, heavens, sea, animals, man, and woman, He said that it was good. All that was created is defined as good. I love driving to work in the morning, because every day, God paints a new picture in the sky that keeps me enamored with His beauty. One day, the sky was different shades of blues and grey, and then to the right, hidden behind fluffy wisps of white clouds, was a brilliant, radiant, glowing light. On another day, the sky had a lavender backdrop with gray wisps of clouds, and the tallest trees touched the tip of the cloud at a deliberate point, as if Da Vinci had painted the sky himself. It was breathtaking. I'm always amazed and end up thinking that the same divine force that created that, created all of us.

The same higher power that takes the time to splash beautiful colors in the sky as easily as a painter throws paint on a canvas made me. Beauty is just good. It's awesome, and it's breathtaking. It just is. That is who we are—beautiful creations that represent the goodness of God. Accept it. Believe it, and embrace your beauty as a unique divine being of the Most High.

The Value of Beauty

The value of beauty is also simple in form; yet we have made it more complicated than it has to be. The value of beauty is intrinsic and extrinsic. We were meant to be internally (intrinsically) good and externally (extrinsically) good. That's it! Since beauty is good and divinely made, then so is its value. If beauty is simple and good, then why does it seem so elusive to some of us? Why do we go through an agonizing struggle to accept our beauty and oneness with all that is good and magnificent?

I believe the struggle to accept our wonderfulness comes from the societal value that is placed on beauty. Beauty is a multibillion dollar industry, because its value is translated into beauty products, clothing, jewelry, cars, sensuality, and sexuality. Images of what we ascribe the meaning of beauty to show up in magazines, on highway placards, on the Internet, and in other visual media. But all of these images are not what beauty means. They are the societal value that is ascribed to what's beautiful, which then causes us to struggle with who we are and were created to be. Until we come to grips with the fact that these manmade values are not the true meaning of beauty, we will always struggle with our identities, and we will have a hard time accepting who we divinely are.

The societal beauty toxins that we breathe and live in make us believe that the intrinsic value of beauty means we must be the life of the party, arrogant, and have all-about-me attitudes. The extrinsic value that society attaches to beauty leads us to believe that to be beautiful, we must have a fashion model's figure, a body builder's muscles, fancy cars, houses, jewelry, etc. Therefore, if we do not have these beautiful things, look like the beautiful images, or act like the beautiful people, then we inaccurately believe that we are not beautiful. We struggle with society's values of beauty and sometime succumb to the horrific notion that we are ugly, not worthy, rejects of all that is beautiful around us. Nothing could be further from the truth!

Accepting Beauty's Extrinsic Value

Let's start with the outward beauty lie first, because it's the one that the world sees and that we readily accept. This lie is so malicious, because it eats away at beauty's intrinsic value. If you believe you are ugly based on society's standard, you feel ugly, and you begin to look ugly. Most of our negative views come from what the world says we look like or should look like. We compare ourselves with magazine models. We dream of being the handsome lead actor or actress in a television show. We marvel at the healthy, glowing hair and skin of the movie stars and wonder why our dull, tired complexions can't look like theirs. We buy their products, take their advice, and secretly wish that we were like them so that we could also be beautiful and perfect. We are bombarded with facial commercials that show us the best soaps, moisturizers, and makeup to use. I've tried some of these products, and many have left me worse off than what I started with in the first place. It's all a bunch of societal garbage that we digest as we deny the natural beauty that we possess.

It's hard not to be sucked into the lie, because the first thing someone usually sees is our outward appearance—namely, our faces. It's also hard not to believe the lie when you are not pleased with your skin or body and you know that they are not what you want them to be. It's hard, for example, when your skin is pimple-prone and you feel less than the beauty you really are. You may not feel beautiful, because you have put on so much weight that your clothes barely fit. How can you embrace the beauty that you are when you are repulsed by yourself because of elements either within or not within your control, such as hormones, medication, or age?

In the girl's gym locker in high school, I watched a girl's face in the mirror as she looked up after she washed her oily skin in the sink. It was an odd moment, because most of the other girls who came

> It's all a bunch of societal garbage that we digest as we deny the natural beauty that we possess.

in and out chuckled and laughed at her. I did something worse. I stared. It was awkward to see someone with bottles of creams and solutions in the girl's bathroom, operating as if she was at home. She looked at me and complimented the smoothness of my skin. She told me how lucky I was not to have acne and proceeded to explain why she had to wash her face with the array of dermatological products displayed on the counter that now looked like a shelf in the pharmacy aisle.

I'll never forget that moment, because I felt awful for her as I stared at the pustules, red blemishes, and dark scars on her shiny skin. Little did I know that I would get adult acne and experience the emotional pain that she must have felt at a very young age. When my face started breaking out, I was in my early twenties. My forehead broke out in a bumpy, pus-filled, horrid mess. I put bangs over it to hide the ugliness and prayed that the wind did not blow my hair and that no one glimpsed at it through my carefully-placed strands. I was embarrassed, and my personality changed. I became more introverted and did not want to be around my peers at work. Compounding my problem was the fact that I did television on-air reporting during that time as well. I found all kinds of blemish-camouflaging products to hide my secret from view. If someone told me then that beauty was only skin-deep, I would have slapped him or her—hard!

If our skin is a mess, then it makes us feel unacceptable and rejected. How can you feel beautiful when you're worried about how your skin looks? Even when my acne went away, after expensive topical creams and dermatological visits, the remnants of shame and embarrassment lingered. Even with clear skin, I felt scarred and uncertain of my beauty. I still did not accept compliments when others said how beautiful I was internally and externally. I thought to myself, *They're just being nice* or *They just want something from me.* How sad!

Recently, I had a Do Me Day—an unannounced self-made holiday that comes at times when I need rejuvenation and restoration. I went to my favorite spa, feeling like a beat-down delivery truck, and came out feeling like a vintage Mercedes Benz. The room smelled of light incense, and the naturalistic sounds of a waterfall and chirping birds filled every corner of the room. The peaceful ambience seeped through me so that when I was called for my facial, I was more than ready for my face to be mushed and mashed like a piece of putty.

In the past, when facials were a part of my dermatological regimen to help extract blackheads, I felt ashamed to have someone look at the bumpy and sometimes painful cystic lesions on my face. Then I sat for thirty minutes in emotional agony, wondering what this clean-faced professional who could have done a skin commercial thought about my imperfect skin. But not this day! This day, my skin was clear, though I had some dark spots from my past. But I didn't care, because I had come full circle, and I felt beautiful. Sure, my skin was clearer than it had ever been, but internally, I had so much love for myself that my face was not my main hang-up or concern.

After feeling so wonderful, I sat back in the waiting room, expecting to be called for my next pleasurable hour of a back massage. As I waited, a friend said, "Your skin is glowing, but ..." I thought, *Brace yourself.* She continued, "You have a red mark on your nose—probably from her extracting a pimple." I didn't go in with a visible pimple on my nose. Maybe there was one coming up, and through the deep massage and heat mask, it rose to a head. In any event, I felt deeply beautiful—an experience I hadn't had in a long time—sitting there with a red mark on the tip of my nose!

There was a time when I would have wanted to crawl under the chair—or better yet, just walk out and stress over why I even thought I deserved a Do Me Day! But I didn't. I surprised myself and laughed! I was at the height of facial perfection, and there was still something imperfect. I told her, "I guess if you turn off the light, it may glow!"

It hurts when our skin is not at its best and doesn't look as smooth as a baby's bottom, but that doesn't mean we are not beautiful! Don't let a pimple steal your joy or a dermatological condition rob you of your right to feel and be beautiful. It may not be easy, but you should concentrate on the beauty and perfection that you are while you work on nursing your skin and body back to their healthiest state of being.

In the meantime, enjoy the journey. Tell yourself—as I eventually learned to tell myself—"I am beautiful!" I am beautiful, whether I have a pimple or a few pimples. I am beautiful, whether you think so or my friend thinks so. I am beautiful, because everything God made is beautiful! I can't say that I've seen an ugly flower or a disgusting sunset. There is beauty

> I am beautiful, because everything that God made is beautiful.

all around me, so why should I not embrace it and believe that I have it? Beauty is not here one moment and gone the next. If something is beautiful, it's beautiful, no matter what the surrounding circumstances. You are beautiful—accept it as who you are. Make the commitment to honor all that you are. Make a commitment to take care of your outward appearance so that you can be the best you possible. That may mean more exercise, more rest, facials, etc. Just be patient with yourself, meet yourself where you are on the journey, and do what you can to bring out all that you are, and you will glow.

Radiating Beauty from Within: Intrinsic Value

Have you ever met a person who was gorgeous on the outside but whose beauty faded when he or she opened his or her mouth? My grandmother often said, "Stop acting so ugly." A person acts ugly when his or her personality is mean-spirited, hurtful, selfish, and vindictive. It does not matter if a person does all he or she can to look good on the outside and adorn God's temple if he or she doesn't take care of the inside. The disciple Peter advised women—specifically, wives—to adorn themselves with humble hearts toward their husbands and not worry about trying to be fancy (1 Peter 3:1–5). I think that can be said for us all. We should not concentrate so much on the extrinsic value of beauty that we forget the intrinsic value. Beauty radiates from within your heart. A beautiful personality and spirit go a long way and show the world how truly confident you are.

Inner beauty lasts much longer than outer beauty, although society emphasizes what's on the outside instead of what is inside of us. Being a person of integrity, excellence, humility, and compassion offers an oasis in a superficial world of must-haves and wannabes. It starts with spending time with yourself, getting to know your likes and dislikes, speaking kind words to yourself, working on your weaknesses, being patient with others, honoring who you are as a child of the Most High, celebrating your accomplishments, and never giving up on the excellent human being that you are and can be.

While you're at it, you might as well stop comparing yourself to other people or even caring about their opinions. That goes for the outside as well as the inside. When you find yourself saying, "I wish I was more like her" or "I wish I was more like him," stop yourself dead in your tracks. You are and can be all that you aspire to be, because you are beautiful—on both the inside and the outside.

We should appreciate all of our attributes and take pride in who we are—both internally and externally. I hope you know from a deep place within you that you are mighty, beautiful, and wondrously made. I pray that you accept that with a conviction that empowers you to move forward confidently and unapologetically in every area of your life. I don't want to spend another day worried about my looks. I just want to relax in the knowledge that I am beautiful. I want to walk like the biblical queens who held their heads high and knew that they were a gift to all creation—not arrogantly, but unquestionably. They rode in their chariots, held up at each corner by strong men, taking in all of their surroundings, inhaling their oneness with all of creation and celebrating their internal and external magnificence.

The Word says that the body is God's temple. In God's temple, there was gold, silver, fine silk, and the best of the land. So it is with our bodies. We should take care of ourselves, which includes eating right, exercise, plenty of fluids, and lots of rest. The old clichés are true: the better you feel, the better you look. You are what you eat. I've learned to deliberately think about what I'm eating, move away from the table when I'm full, go to sleep when I'm sleepy, and exercise even when I don't feel like it. Joyce Meyer, pastor of Joyce Meyer Ministries in Fenton, Missouri, says it best: you have to do things on purpose. Some things we may not like or love to do, but they are good for us. They were meant to maintain us and keep us beautiful—so do them. Take care of your beautiful self.

Embracing Beauty

Dear reader, my gift to you is a reminder of what you already are: *beautiful.* You are beautiful from the time you get up in the morning until the time you lie down at night. You are precious and worthy to be adored and admired like a rose bulb sitting in a glass. You are exquisite and divinely made on the inside and outside. Stop criticizing your looks. Stop doubting yourself. You are beautiful in every way. Please don't forget it. Enjoy it! Embrace it. Own it. It is you—it always has been and always will be!

Embrace Your Beauty

Beautiful Affirmations

- I am beautiful, because I am me.
- I am beautiful, because I am the divine representation of God.
- I am beautiful—just because.
- I am beautiful, because everything in the universe reflects who I am.
- I am beautiful today, I will be tomorrow, and I was yesterday, too.
- I love my weight, because I'm a work in progress.
- I love the skin that I am in.
- I love who I am.
- I love myself.
- I love all that I am and all that I am capable of becoming.

Beauty Essentials

- Get to bed on time.
- Exercise.
- Be on time.
- Eating right.
- Monitor your finances.
- Stay away from excess. (Be disciplined.)
- Have a prayer life.
- Spend time with family and friends.

Scripture Reflection

For you created my inmost being; you knit me together in my mother's womb. I praise you because I am fearfully and wonderfully made; your works are wonderful, I know that full well.

—Psalm 139:13–14

Journal Notes: Embrace Your Beauty

Look at yourself in the mirror. Say the beauty affirmations listed on the previous page for a week. Then answer the questions below.

1. What messages do you tell yourself daily? Are they different from the beauty affirmations you recited this week?

2. How can you embrace the beauty affirmations every day?

3. How can you honor yourself more than you do?

4. Look at the beauty essentials. Write down two that you will consistently work on this week. How did they make you feel?

5. Take five minutes to look at something beautiful. Please describe it and how it made you feel.

6. List five of your internal attributes that you appreciate.

7. List five of your external attributes that you appreciate.

8. How can you show yourself how much you appreciate your beauty on both the inside and the outside?

9. What was the most defining message from this chapter? How will you implement it into my life?

Remember, you are beautifully made. Don't forget it! Enjoy it! Embrace it! It is you!

CHAPTER 6

Accept Your Abundance

She had struggled for most of her life to survive with her two children. After divorcing her husband, she went on welfare and got financial assistance from local organizations. She went to college in order to make a better life for herself and years later ended up working for me. She did not make the effort to dress for work, saying that she could not afford it. She used all of her leave time as soon as she earned it, saying she deserved it. She called credit cards her mom and dad, saying she needed them. She never had a savings plan, so when her roof needed repairs, she covered it with tarp and waited until she could afford it. She was the first one in line to get her W-2 form, because she needed to file her taxes to pay off her credit card bill that she had just used to purchase furniture. She said she didn't think that she could afford to retire; although she was almost sixty years old, she planned to work for the rest of her life.

I didn't understand why she never seemed to have enough. At

first, I thought that it was her low salary, so I provided her with opportunities to earn more. But that didn't change her financial situation. Then I thought it was because she was a single woman trying to take care of her children and grandchildren, but she shared that she received assistance from the state. She received financial support for medical care, child care, and food. Next, I thought she didn't have accrued time because she was sickly, but then I monitored the days she took off, and most were for personal use. She took a few hours here and a few hours there. She had a pattern of rarely working a full week. When she was actually sick, she was on leave without pay. She said she could never take a vacation but seemed bewildered as to why. Finally, I overheard her say to a coworker that she accepted that this was her lot in life. She said, "I will never have anything." Then I got it. She was crippled by the spirit of lack.

When you adopt this spirit of lack, it takes over in every aspect of your life. It is like the root of a poisonous plant that seeps into fertile soil and insidiously grows. Its branches take on the form of lack of time, money, energy, creativity, motivation, and belief. Its roots strangle your will to be financially free and leave you in a codependent relationship with *can't, won't,* and *didn't.* It suffocates the voice of financial freedom and manifests itself in how you dress, what you think, and what you say about who you are and the possibilities for your future.

Accepting your abundance is just the opposite. It allows you to reconnect with your core being and believe that your circumstances can and will change as long as you latch on to the truth that you are meant to have more than enough. Embracing abundance is more than a financial plan. It is a mindset. It's a belief that you have the right to be prosperous and have your assets (gifts, creativity, finances, relationships, wardrobe, etc.) increased! It is making a decision to demand that life gives you all that you are owed and then some. It's shaking off the belief that you are stuck in a financial abyss from which there is no hope of return.

I love the book of Exodus because it tells a magnificent yet simple story. The magnificence is in the inexplicable stream of plagues, the powerful wonder of the parting Red Sea, the incomprehensible pillar of fire, and the miraculous raining of bread and meat from heaven. But the simplicity is in the love a Father has in providing for His struggling, beaten, and broken-spirited children who were used as slaves in Egypt. When God sent them out of Egypt, He could have just told them to go and not look back. He could have told them to go and take only what they had with them. But no, that's not how the God of abundance acts! Aren't you glad about it? Say "Amen" if you can!

When the Israelites left Egypt, God told them to not only take what they had, but He also sent them with all the Egyptians had! Exodus 12:35–36 says, "The Israelites did as Moses instructed and asked the Egyptians for articles of silver and gold and for clothing. The Lord had made the Egyptians favorably disposed toward the people, and they gave them what they asked for; so they plundered the Egyptians." God rewarded these former slaves, His children, with wealth! Why would God do that? He wanted them to know that they were worthy of abundance. He wanted them to start a new beginning, knowing that they deserved all the riches that their hearts and hands could hold. The Egyptians gave them all—not some, not most, but *all*—that they required. That day, He freed them not only from bondage, but also a mindset of defeat and lack. He grabbed the spirit of lack by its root and said, "No more."

God wants that for all of us. Before you can imagine yourself out of debt and financially free, you must embrace abundance in your thinking. You must change your mindset! You must be aware of what you think about your finances, how you present yourself to others, and what you do with what you have been given. Before you can think about having a zero balance on that high-interest credit card, you have to uproot the spirit of lack and say, "No more." Stop it from growing and replicating in the garden of hope and prosperity that you are trying to create. Accept the truth that you can have all that you desire as long as you stay on the path toward financial freedom.

A Road to Financial Freedom

Let me start with a disclaimer: I am not a financial guru or accountant—not by any stretch of the imagination. I love math and can balance a checkbook, but that is the sum total of my affiliation with numbers. What I am, though, is a person who has had a miraculous yet painful experience of getting out of debt. I have gone through the ubiquitous affliction called financial craziness. It has left me wiser, in harmony with myself and my finances, and grateful for the experience. I am now financially healthier and more committed than ever to embracing my divine calling to be abundant, financially free, and at peace with prosperity.

You may be like I once was, fluctuating from one end of the crazy financial spectrum to another. One minute, I was spending more than I could afford while lying to myself by saying things like, "I'll pay it off when the bill comes in," knowing good and well that would be within three months to a year. Financial craziness occurs when you are in disharmony with the divine nature of abundance. It's caused by not knowing your true worth while simultaneously disrespecting the value of money to provide you with your needs and then lying to yourself about your condition.

Financial craziness goes against God's plan for us. Jeremiah 29:11 tells us that God says, "For I know the plans I have for you ... plans to prosper you and not to harm you, plans to give you hope and a future." Jesus also stated that He came that we might have life and have it more abundantly (John 10:10). Think about it—what purpose does it serve God for us to remain financially crippled? He would rather be glorified when we walk into our divine abundance.

It's too bad I didn't think about that when I went through my own financial bout of craziness. I bought a white plastic fence to keep my former neighbor's eight miniature pinschers off my lawn. Instead of having a conversation with her, I put myself $3,000 in debt, knowing that I would be unable to pay that off with my teacher's salary, since I barely made enough to pay the household bills. I paid for materials and labor costs just to install a fence on one half of my property! The neighbor moved a month or so later, and I still had the $3,000 bill plus interest and a fence on half of my property. That's financially crazy!

It gets better. I use to walk up and down the department store aisles, looking for items on sale. I'd buy things on sale using the store credit card, and by the time I paid for them, the cost for the items was more than the sale price, because I paid additional interest. I not only wasted my time, but also an opportunity to save money. I was even generous enough to give the savings back to the department store with interest. How crazy is that?

Perhaps you have tormented yourself on occasion by depriving yourself of simple pleasures, finding excuses like "I don't deserve that," "I can get that later," or "I can use this money for the kids, house, etc." In those instances, I wished deeply that I could get the thing, think about going back to the store and getting the thing, and talk to my friends about why I didn't deserve the thing, knowing that I wouldn't get the thing. Then when I'd convince myself to just stop in the store to see the thing to add to my torment, the thing would then not be on the rack anymore, and then I would say, "That's proof I didn't need the thing." That's crazy! Now what I do is save money for myself to buy (within reason) things that give me pleasure and make me feel good about myself. It took a while to get there, though, because I was financially imbalanced and crippled by the spirit of lack.

You may be afflicted with financial craziness if you have some of these symptoms:

- You live paycheck to paycheck without a plan or hope for the future.

- The credit card company owns your paycheck before you even earn one.

- You fall victim to every whimsical buying spree.

- You hold your breath at the cash register, praying that the transaction will be approved on the over-the-limit credit card. Then when it's not, you look at the cashier and say,

"*Hmm,* something must be wrong with the card. Here, try this one."

- You have never asked for a raise or looked for another job to earn more income.

- You purchase items on your credit card, knowing that you can't afford to pay for them in full when the bill is due.

- You do not have a retirement plan or savings.

- You do not have an emergency fund but rely on the great hope that you will not have any financial challenges in your lifetime.

- You plan for your children to go to college, but you have your fingers crossed that they will be able to get enough scholarships to pay for the tuition, moving costs, academic fees, and books. You may also wish that they get enough summer jobs during high school to cover all the costs.

- You write a check when you are not sure that you have the funds but knowing that they will be covered by your overdraft plan, which charges more interest than your high-interest credit cards.

If you can relate to any of the above symptoms, don't feel bad, because at one time or another, I could relate to them, too. Since then, I've learned to embrace abundance. I have no time or room in my life to entertain financial craziness. I *choose* to be financially whole. I *choose* to be financially free. And I *choose* to be financially secure and at peace with what I have, who I am, and what I would like to achieve.

Financial Freedom: A Choice

To be honest with you, all of my life, I thought that getting out of debt was something that other people were able to do. I read the success stories, listened to the how-tos, and wrote down "Get out of debt" at the top of my New Year's resolution list. On the surface, I thought it could happen for me, but deep down inside, I didn't believe it. That's why I continued to sabotage myself by buying things I could not afford and putting my financial future in the hands of the credit card holders who charged high interest rates that left me with a lifetime sentence of indebtedness.

I will tell you what I did to get out of debt; however, I encourage you to read personal finance books to receive more support and financial expertise. My goal is only to show you that it *is* possible to get out of debt and to become financially free! It *is* possible to reclaim the financial freedom you had when you were born when you owed no one and the world was yours for the asking! It *is* possible to choose your financial destiny as long as you are willing to go through the process to wipe your slate clean!

The Process

Decide to be financially free. Whatever steps you choose to become financially secure, the first step has to be to make a decision and commitment to yourself to become financially free, no matter how uncomfortable it may be. There is a difference between financial freedom and getting out of debt. You can get out of debt but still be trapped by your lifestyle, poor spending habits, lack of planning, and disconnection with your past relationships with money.

I spent years trying to get out of debt. I read books, listened to financial gurus, and was still in debt. It was only when I decided to be financially free that my circumstances began to change. I equated being financially free with getting back to my true nature of not belonging to a company, credit card, income bracket, or lifestyle. I got tired of owing. I felt inadequate—as if I was not enough and did not have enough—and I wanted desperately to reconnect with feeling whole and at peace with my finances.

I got tired of the anxiety I felt when the utility bills came in and I hoped that I had enough to pay them. I no longer wanted to worry about whether or not my cable would be cut off because I didn't pay it so that I could pay another bill. (I did what my grandmother called *robbing Peter to pay Paul*.) When you get to that place, saying, "I want to get out of debt" is just not enough. I had to change the way that I did things, understand why I did them, and strive for a greater goal of being in control of my finances, emotions, and destiny.

Multibillionaire Tony Robbins is known worldwide for his energetic self-empowerment seminars. He has written dozens of self-help books. But what is most fascinating about him is that he started with little income. He was broke and living in a one-bedroom apartment. He talks about getting tired of being broke and deciding that he was meant to have more. That's what motivated him to start studying success. He made a decision not to be broke anymore and began a process of embracing wealth. He worked diligently to find out how successful people thought and what they did differently, and he copied them. He made a decision to break free and then committed to the process.

Commit to the process. After I decided that I wanted to be financially free, I had to commit to do whatever it took (within reason) to accomplish that goal. I had to write down and keep myself accountable for every dime that came in and every dime that went out. I began by tracking my expenses and keeping a budget. I did my best not to go over my budget on a weekly basis, and when I did, I tried to compensate by spending less in another area. For example, if I budgeted $75.00 for food one week and the gas bill came in $10.00 more than expected, then I'd only have $65.00 for food. With that $65.00, I would make sure I stretched every penny using coupons or going to different supermarkets for buy-one-get-one-free (BOGO) sales.

I disciplined myself not to shop whimsically but with a purpose. I stopped going out on Sundays for breakfast, eating at our favorite family restaurant every other week, and stopping into stores "just to see what was on sale." Usually, when I went for a "go see," I ended up walking out of the store with things that I didn't need. Instead, I looked for the sales in the newspaper advertisements and flyers. If there was something that I needed or wanted, then I went to look with a purpose and walked out with just that item. I retrained my eyes not to see other sales or things I thought I needed.

I told my daughter that we were on a budget, so she had to stop asking, "Mommy, can I have this?" every time we went shopping. Although I usually said no, it complicated my plan, because I'd start weighing whether she needed it. If I thought she did, I'd get it and think about what in the basket I needed to take out in order to stay on budget. It took commitment, discipline, hard work, and family support. I shocked myself with how committed I was to the process—which, over time, became easier to handle.

The most important thing I learned about being committed to the process was to believe what comedian George Lopez says: "You can do it!" I developed much financial confidence, because I made little decisions every day that added up to my financial goal. I felt in control of my spending, finances, and life. Sure, there were things that I did not get at first that I truly wanted, but the bigger picture was that I ended up being financially free to get those things later when I could afford them.

Discover your financial gene code. We all have what I call a "financial gene code." It's what our parents passed on to us—either verbally or nonverbally—about money and financial management. They picked up their clues from their parents, who got their ideas from theirs. The financial gene code has messages that dictate our relationship with money. Once we understand our financial gene codes, we are able to understand why we make the decisions we make, and we can learn to make more informed choices about how to manage our funds.

I approached the research on my financial gene code by asking myself why I had developed a pattern of paying off debt, spending, getting back into debt, not saving, and then worrying about my financial future. I had to explore my version of financial craziness and find out how and why I got to the place of indebtedness. I explored when I relinquished my financial freedom and why and what I needed to do to safeguard myself from letting that happen again.

My maternal grandmother never had money. She grew up poor in Panama, where she worked as a maid to make ends meet for her four children. My grandfather also worked; however, he spent his money on alcohol, leaving my grandmother to scrounge around for food for the family. She told stories of the neighbors in the building bringing food for her and her children to eat. She reminisced about cooking soup to stretch the food for all of them and giving her children bread with butter for breakfast. My aunts told stories of picking fruits from trees because they were so hungry or showing up at godmothers' houses right before dinner time.

My grandmother came to the United States and worked in a sheet music factory for many years; she also sold numbers and spent her money on cigarettes. I remember her talking about not having enough money and always owing on credit cards. My mother, however, fared much better. She went to nursing and business schools. She was able to save money and sent money home to Panama to help her family. However, after my parents divorced, my mother was left to raise me and my brother on her income alone for many years in New York until she received minimal child support years later.

Growing up with a single mother who had to work two jobs to make ends meet, I watched my mom put needed expenses on credit cards in order to make it. My mother took my brother and me to Bloomingdales every so often for bagels and turkey sandwiches. Boy, what a treat for us! The bread was so soft that it melted in our mouths, and the turkey was fresh and sweet— nothing like the salty, slimy packaged brands. Little did I know that she took us for a treat, because Bloomingdales was the only credit card she had available to charge for us to get a meal! Can you imagine?

I saw my mother crying over bills and selling everything in our house, including colored hangers and mismatched towels. She worked on the weekends at the church rectory. We loved Sundays at the church rectory, because while the priests ate their dinner in the dining room, we were able to eat the same prime rib and sirloin steak in the kitchen. We thought it was another treat, but actually, it was another way for my mother to make ends meet and provide us with a delicious Sunday dinner.

As children, we always had what we needed, but we knew that we shouldn't burden our mother by asking for more. Christmas was always overdone, with us getting every toy in the Sears Christmas Wish Book. I'm not sure how my mother managed to do that, but I'm sure it was on a Sears credit card. Later in life, she admitted that she did not want us to not have a good Christmas, even though she could not afford it. We also couldn't afford private school, but both my brother and I went to private schools from elementary school through college.

The financial lesson that I learned from my mother was to get a good education in order to fight against poverty; make sacrifices to give your children all that they need and possibly want, even if you can't afford it; live above your means; don't save for rainy days; and use your credit cards to get you through the rough times. I also learned from her to spend on quality items; don't be cheap when it comes to treating yourself; and God will help you, but He really has nothing to do with your finances—work, pray, and work some more.

My father's side of the family came from humble beginnings as well. My paternal grandfather was a preacher, and he also worked in an auto shop. He believed in education and encouraged his family to go to school. Growing up on farms in the South taught him the value of hard work and a good education. He moved his family to Virginia for a better way of life and encouraged his brother's family to do the same. My dad worked hard, went to college, and even served in the military. My dad saved dollars and coins. He has a jar for this and a jar for that. I believe he learned from his family the old adage, "Every little bit helps." He believed that you should recycle everything from paper to old tennis shoes. I got old things from the Lost and Found from my dad when I was growing up and rarely received anything new unless it was Christmas time.

I learned from my dad frugality, to save a dollar at a time, and to recycle, because everything has a use. My parents never told me any of this, because neither of them spoke to me about money management or financial security. I really did not know what it meant to be financially free. I only knew the lessons that I gleaned from what they did. Once I dissected the root of my financial beliefs, I was able to see where I was going wrong. I made a commitment to change my beliefs and stick to my decision to become financially free no matter what I had to do (within moral reason).

From my financial gene code, I realized the root of my aversion to abundance. My family tried to make ends meet and believed that education leads to prosperity and success. From the Great Depression to the Civil Rights Movement, they adopted messages that then transferred to me. My financial gene code taught me the following messages:

- To avoid poverty, you must get a good education.

- Live above your means, as it's a way of life.

- Put everything you can't afford on a credit card.

- Scrimp dollars and change in order to save.

- Abundance is just a picture in a magazine and is not for you.

- You will always have to juggle your expenses just to make it day to day.

- God is not in your finances, but He'll "make a way" so you can keep your head above water.

My parents didn't say these things, but this is what I understood as a child. In any event, all of these are lies from the pit of hell that at one time kept me trapped and financially immobile.

I now tell myself,

- To avoid poverty, you must embrace your abundance.

- Live below your means so that you can save more for the future. (Thank you, Suze Orman!)

- When you charge something on a credit card, be able to pay for it when the bill is due. If you can't afford it, don't buy it.

- Save enough money to provide an emergency fund for yourself.

- Abundance defines who you are and is reflected in everything around you.

- Be wise with how you spend your money, and be in control of every dollar that comes in and goes out.

- God is in your finances, and He'll make a way for you to prosper beyond your wildest dreams.

These truths have helped me on my road to financial freedom, and I truly hope they help you.

Get a plan, and stick to it. Armed with this understanding, I made a financial plan. It included my short-term and long-term goals. I had weekly, monthly, biannual, and annual goals that would help me become financially free. I decided that I didn't just want to get out of debt and stay out of debt, but I also wanted to be free from all of the lies I had told myself over the years. I wanted to finally accept my financial destiny and get back to being whole again. I got a plan and stood by my plan, no matter how difficult it was in the beginning.

As part of my plan, I rewarded myself for my milestones. When I paid the bill down to a certain mark, I got my favorite movie from the library, popped popcorn, and had a treat. Sometimes I spent money on a two-for-one ice cream cone deal or a half-price vanilla milkshake. My milestones were always inexpensive and either free or almost free so that I could stay on my budget diet. But after reaching several milestones, I did not need to reward myself anymore, because I was so excited that the debt was getting lower. Seeing the numbers decline was such an unbelievable experience that I took pleasure in that alone.

I also consolidated debt by taking advantage of the cards that allowed you to pay off the total in one to two years. This helped me, because under those promotions, the customer doesn't have to pay interest on the card until the promotion expires. However, the catch is that once the promo expires and you do not pay the amount, the credit card company may charge you interest that accrued from the date the promo began. If you go this route, be careful, and have a plan to pay it off before the promo expires. If you do not pay it off, the credit card company says, "Gotcha." The company also charges a processing fee upfront. Depending on your debt amount, you'll have to weigh whether or not it's worth it.

For me, it was worth it. I remember the day I paid off the last credit card. I planned to have a personal party. I thought I'd go to the salon and get a mani-pedi and a facial! I thought that I'd be ecstatic, but surprisingly, I wasn't. It surprised me how nonchalant I was at paying off the debt. Maybe I felt that way because I had celebrated the milestones of success. It felt surreal. I was keenly aware of a feeling of peace with myself and my money. I felt like I'd reached the finish line in a race. I knew that I would make it, even though it was hard, but I knew I did not want to run the same race again. I felt like a heavy burden was lifted!

I breathed deeply, smiled, and walked away from the computer after making my last online payment, knowing that I was finally financially free. The money that God granted me to have was finally mine and did not belong to any of the credit card holders or student loan lenders. It felt good knowing that my paychecks were no longer spent already! Even though I could afford a Do Me Day with a mani-pedi and facial, it didn't seem necessary to spend the money. I was just proud of being in a good place financially—finally!

Be grateful. During this process, I started to keep a gratitude journal. In this journal, I'd write down five things I was grateful for in my life. I wrote something new every day. I began to realize how blessed I was to have my health, family, friends, hot water, food to eat, a job, etc. I began to appreciate those things even more, and I became content with my life and with myself. I no longer felt the stress and heaviness of not having enough financially, because I knew that I had so much to be thankful for that I had no room for ingratitude.

I had credit card debt, but each day, I had the ability to decide to get out of it. Sure, I didn't buy everything I wanted, but I truly had everything that I needed. My attitude of gratitude was bolstered by Deuteronomy 8:3–4. God reminded the ungrateful Jews that He provided for them in the desert by giving them manna to eat, and He made sure that their clothes did not get old or their shoes wear out for their forty-year journey—a journey that should have taken them eleven days instead of forty years had they been grateful and not complained about everything.

What inspired me is that God took care of the Israelites in the desert. All of their needs were met. He may not have given them fancy food or new clothes, but they had what they needed without working for it. I became even more grateful for my shoes that were not fancy but got me through for a few years. I loved my old suits even more. I had not bought a new suit in two years because of my debt-reduction plan, but the ones I had were still sharp, and I was still able to afford to send them to the dry cleaners.

The more that I became grateful for what I had, the more financial blessings took hold in my life. I began to get financial opportunities and ideas that I never had before to help keep my costs down and my income flow increasing. Being grateful made me content. It put me at peace with myself, and I began to concentrate on God's goodness and mercy. I had made financial mistakes, and He still kept me all of these years. That's a blessing that can't be calculated in dollars and cents. Like Paul, I learned to be content when I was down and now that I'm not. I learned to be at peace by remaining grateful for all that I had. My life was no longer measured by the balance on the credit card bill but the abundance of love, prosperity, creativity, and peace in my life.

Give! Give, no matter how hard it may be when you are trying to pay off debt. Give your time. Give your old clothes. Give your heart. Give some of your money. You have to give in order to receive. This was a principle that I tried to ignore, but I couldn't. When you are grateful for all that you have, you must give to others. I believe that is our only mission here on this planet—to love one another and give the gifts that God gave us to share.

You may not find this easy to do at first, because the cycle of debt keeps you in the mentality of lack. However, when you open your hand, more comes into it for you to give. God put us here to be able to help one another. Aaron helped Moses, Samuel helped Elijah, Ruth helped Naomi, Esther helped her people, and Simon of Cyrene helped the Son of God carry His cross to Calvary. We are here to support one another and give to each other what we can.

Don't block your blessings. Being humble, helpful, and kind-hearted helps to nurture the ground for prosperity to grow. You will not receive when you are ugly to other people or when you hurt them. If you are to truly receive blessings, then you shouldn't do things to block them from coming to you.

One day, I walked into Walmart to get a few items early in

the morning. I deliberately went out of my way to say hello to the greeter, smile at those in the grocery aisle, and compliment the cashier. On my way out, I went to purchase a soda from the vending machine, and a supplier was filling another machine close by. As luck would have it, the soda machine would not take my dollar. The supplier came over to help. He opened the machine, gave me a soda, and told me to keep my dollar! It was just a dollar, but I believe that I received a blessing because I was a blessing to others. If you don't believe me, just try it for a month, and see what blessings you receive in return for all that you give. They may not be monetary blessings, but I can assure you that you will open the door to abundance in many areas of your life.

My financial victory is yours, too, because you can do what I did and do it better! It doesn't matter how much debt you're in. Yesterday's decisions and mistakes are in the past. Today is a new day—a day that breathes abundance and prosperity into you that will manifest in your finances and relationships. They will renew your commitment to getting out of debt and staying out of financial bondage. Say to yourself, *This is a new day. It's my day to be financially free.*

> Today is a new day. It's a day that breathes abundance and prosperity into you that will manifest in your finances and relationships.

If you still don't believe that financial freedom is within your reach, look outside your window. There is not a lack of birds, sky, wind, people, etc. God doesn't operate in a realm of lack. I love Psalm 23. It's read at funerals all the time, and I thought that was why so many people loved it, because it speaks about God laying us down in a pasture of peace and us dwelling in His kingdom. But I love it because it speaks about God's abundance and good will toward us. "The Lord is my shepherd, I lack nothing." I shall not want for any good thing. He is the shepherd who takes care of me and all of my needs. "He makes me lie down in green pastures. He leads me beside quiet waters." It doesn't say that the pasture is withered, yellow grass or a meadow with patches in it. No, it's a green, plush pasture that he lays us down in peace. "He refreshes my soul." As a shepherd, He takes me to a peaceful place where He restores me and prepares me for greatness and abundance. "Even though I walk through the darkest valley, I will fear no evil, for you are with me." Yes, though I walk through shadows of lack, despair, and debt, I will not fear, because the God of abundance and all good who is all-knowing is with me. "Your rod and your staff, they comfort me." That's what a good shepherd does. He uses a rod and staff to guide his sheep and give them a sense of security. I am secure around God, because like the good shepherd, He only wants what is good for me.

"You prepare a table before me in the presence of my enemies." In front of lack, doubt, degradation, and poverty, God put me at a table with food and abundance. He shows my enemies that I am meant to have more! "You anoint my head with oil; my cup overflows." God blesses me! I have more than enough! "Surely, your goodness and love will follow me all the days of my life, and I will dwell in the house of the Lord forever." I will have only goodness, grace, abundance, and mercy all of my life, and I will dwell in God's house of abundance, love, and goodness forever.

I want to shout from the mountain top that you and I were

made to be abundant! We are supposed to have more than enough—a cup that runs over! I don't need that when I die! I need abundance now! I need to know that I am more than enough, and I have more than enough now.

If you do not feel this way, then just say, "I'm working on it. I'm working on feeling abundant. I'm working on accepting my abundance. My abundance is coming! I'm grateful for my abundance!" God is not a God of lack. He told Adam and Eve to be fruitful and multiply; He gave Abraham land, animals, and a nation; He made Noah pack the ark with every beast of the land and air; He anointed Joseph's head with oil and gave him favor. Joseph became second in command to Pharaoh. God had Pharaoh give the Israelites all of the gold their hearts desired; He told Moses to build His tabernacle out of the finest materials; He gave Job double for his trouble; He brought Ruth from poverty to riches when she married Boaz; He made a lowly shepherd boy named David the King of Israel.

God is a God of abundance, not lack. You are a descendant of abundance, not debt. You are made to be financially free, not broken down by financial despair. If you don't believe what I say, fake it! Tell yourself that your streak of abundance is coming. Tell yourself that you are meant to have more than you can handle—so much that you will have to give some away!

EMBRACING THE MESSAGE

Accepting Your Abundance

🍃 Decide to be financially free.

🍃 Commit to the process.

🍃 Discover your financial gene code.

🍃 Get a plan, and stick to it.

🍃 Be grateful.

🍃 Give!

🍃 Don't block your blessings.

Scripture Reflection

Ask and it will be given to you; seek and you will find; knock and the door will be opened to you.

—Matthew 7:7

Journal Notes: Accepting Your Abundance

The exercises below may help put you in the frame of mind to receive your abundance. As you go through each one, please be patient with yourself. If you are in debt, like I was, remember that coming out of debt does not occur overnight. It will take some time to undo some of the decisions you made to get yourself in debt and back on the road to financial harmony.

1. If you have not done this already, write down your monthly income and your monthly expenses. Take a critical look at each area to see if you can reduce your expenses (entertainment, cable, phone, etc.). If you are able to reduce in those areas, put your savings into an interest-bearing account, or pay more down on a current bill.

2. Before you go shopping, write down a list of items to buy. Look through newspapers and magazines for sales and coupons. Discipline yourself not to deviate from your list when you go to the store. If you impulsively pick something up to buy, ask yourself, "Do I need this item, or do I want it?"

   a. If you *need* the item, then ask yourself, "Can I do without it for another two weeks, when I can include it in my budget?" If the answer is no, then ask yourself, "What can I take off my current list to stay within my budget?"

   b. If you *want* the item, then ask yourself, "Can I do without it for another two weeks, when I can include it in my budget?" If the answer is no, then ask yourself, "Why do I want this? Is it because it is just here? Is it because I am rewarding myself? If I am rewarding myself, then can I plan a way to reward myself within my budget?"

3. Check the interest on all of your credit card bills. Call the credit card companies, and ask if they are able to lower your interest rate.

4. Take time to congratulate yourself for at least making an attempt to change your old spending habits. Embracing abundance is more about your frame of mind and willingness to accept another way of life than the bottom line in your bank account.

5. Embrace your family. Do something special with the ones you love. It could be as simple as watching television and eating a bag of movie butter popcorn.

6. Thank God that you are alive and still here to celebrate life.

7. Keep a gratitude journal. Be thankful for simple things, like being able to have a bag lunch at work. Some people in the world can't even afford that. The more you are grateful for, the more you will receive, and the less you will stress out about your checkbook.

Remember, the road to financial freedom begins one step at a time. Take your step until you are able to run laps around financial despair and lack!

CHAPTER 7

Be Open to Love: Making Room for Goodness

As the sun steps down from its daily post, its rays stream across the crystal-blue ocean, creating a gloss over the rippling waves. The gentle breeze glides along the rustling palm trees that cast a loving shadow on the couple below. Barefooted on the warm sand, they stand enchanted as the wind gently whips her lilac lace dress and whimsically dishevels her hair. Slowly, he reaches to wipe the glistening tear that traced a line through the make-up on her cheek; readily, she takes his hand and locks his fingers in hers. A gold glimmering band peeks through. The shadow from the palm tree innocently sways, their invited guests sigh, and the couple exchanges a tender kiss. Their audience applauds; the waves crash against the shore, and the summer wind playfully dances with the tiger lilies in her bouquet.

This image is beautiful, isn't it? It's a typical romantic scene in which two become one, because they have opened their hearts to loving each other for eternity. It's a scene that I've played over in my head a few times. I think it may be the backdrop for my next trip down the aisle. But before I was even ready to accept that image as a possibility, I had to open myself up to love.

I'm not talking about opening up to a man loving me; I'm talking about opening myself up to loving myself and being able to accept the love of another. It's an openness that only comes from knowing that I am already loved and therefore can only be loveable to someone else.

Love is what it is. It doesn't have to prove itself. It doesn't have to do anything to be what it is. Love is a knowledge that you belong to something greater than yourself. It is the acceptance that you are part of a greater purpose that reflects love in everything that it does. For example, bears love honey. No one had to convince them to love honey. They did not have to learn to love honey. They just do. It's natural. What about a lioness and her cub? She loves her cub.

On the Discovery Channel the other night, I watched, gripping my chest, as a mother lion tried to save her cub from the king of the pride. He took her cub to eat, and this mother lion tried to free her cub from him. When she realized that she could not steal her cub away or distract the male lion from his pernicious mission, she looked on helplessly, as if pleading with the male lion to let her cub go. He didn't, and she slowly went away with her head bowed down. Her love was just natural. She didn't love the cub because it did anything or tried to prove itself to her. She loved it just because it was hers.

After nine months of weight gain, exhaustion, and bloating, mothers have to push out a slimy thing that causes pain throughout their whole bodies until it's delivered. But when a mother sees her child, the natural love overflows. There's no more pain—just a giving and natural connection. Love is what it is.

Love is not ashamed of itself. It does not hide under a bush. It is there for all to see. Love does not cower but stands in the face of fear. Love does not criticize itself, hold grudges, or harbor regrets. Love doesn't make excuses but moves forward with life, self-accepting, undaunted, and determined. Love sacrifices, gives, hopes, laughs, provides, sings, restores, embraces, encourages, cries, endures, understands, remembers, creates, exists, stands, waits, trusts, supports, respects, conquers, rebuilds, carries, mourns, engages, triumphs, reignites, rectifies, moves, rests, accepts, talks, listens, feeds, plans, dances, climbs, excels, caresses, responds, stands firm, honors, ignites, prevents, depends, and forgives.

Paul divinely defined the depth of love thousands of years ago. While sitting alone in a prison, waiting to be executed, he wrote in his letter to the Corinthians, "Love is patient, love is kind. It does not envy, it does not boast, it is not proud. It does not dishonor others, it is not self-seeking, it is not easily angered, and it keeps no record of wrongs. Love does not delight in evil, but rejoices with the truth. It always protects, always trusts, always hopes, always preserves. Love never fails" (1 Corinthians 13:4–8).

> *Love doesn't make excuses but moves forward with life, self-accepting, undaunted, and determined.*

There were years when I did not believe that, even though they were part of the scriptural readings at my wedding. I came to believe that love was not patient but accusatory. It was not kind but selfish. It envied, boasted, and was self-seeking. It was easily angered and frustrated and recorded all of my mistakes and wrongs. And when I gave love back, it resembled what I had received. My love did not protect, trust, hope, or preserve. I failed to show love, because what I thought love was had failed me time and time again.

I was always disappointed, confused, and hurt by what I thought was love. Then I thought that being loved was what love was all about. I knew that my family loved me, and I believed that God may have had some type of affection for me, since He created me. But I did not know what it meant to be open to the love. I did not know that I was just a magnet to which love was attracted. I thought love was something I had to earn, do, and horde, because I might not get more like it in my lifetime. I thought love was part of a routine, part of what was expected—humdrum and boring. I thought it was doing things that I was asked to do even if I did not want to do them.

Then love was proof that I was committed to a man I thought I loved. It was doing things to prove my commitment. That meant that love was never tired. It kept going without being replenished and restored. It was always giving in and receiving nothing but the inner knowledge that I was proving my love. It meant putting myself last all the time and questioning God and my marriage most of the time. It meant not being my true self, not being open to goodness, and not accepting all the good that was meant for me. That's not love at all. It's a distorted image of love from a broken mirror created by years of lies and closing oneself off to the gift that love always brings.

The Gift of Love

Being open to love begins with accepting the gift of loving yourself for yourself. As we discussed in the second chapter, it begins with embracing the gift that something greater has made you and has a purpose for your life. It means receiving the gift that you are loved not for what you can do or prove but for who you are—a unique, beautiful representation of all that is good, loving, and kind. It took me a while to accept this gift, because I was so busy trying to show love, be love, and have love. I did not accept love. *When you can love yourself, then and only then can you be open to love.* Think about that for a moment.

Do you accept the love that is around you? I don't mean accepting an expression of love like a hug or a gift from a friend. These things are comforting and appreciated, but if you do not accept love, it's like receiving a beautifully wrapped empty box that is beautiful on the outside but carries no connection, because there's nothing on the inside. Do you accept the love that is a part of the breath that rises each time your chest does, blinks every time your eyelids blink, and beats every time your heart moves to its own inner rhythm, sustaining your life flow?

Do you criticize yourself? Do you put yourself down? Do you think you are not able to do what you are talented at doing? Do you hover in fear? Are you crippled by doubt? Do you not like some part of your body? Do you compare yourself to others? Do you regret your life decisions? Do you not like what you see in the mirror? Do you have habits or addictions that hide who you are and what you are called to do? Do you go all the time and not find time to rest? Do you believe everything others say about you? Have you pushed love away? Have you shied away from finding time to accept love? Ultimately, do you, dear reader, accept the love that is all around you?

To be open to love means doing away with all of the comparisons, self-criticism, and self-deprivation life forces you to swallow. It means having the courage to accept love for what it is. It's making a decision to step out of the rain and into the sunshine. Remove your tattered rain coat that is dripping wet and weighed down with regrets. Close your protective umbrella that says to love, "You can't touch me while I hide under here." Step into the new day of letting love pour over you, renewing you with a new outlook on what love is. Accept this as the gift you have been given just because you are you. It's not a gift you have to put on layaway or prove that you deserve. It is just there for the asking and receiving.

Receive Love's Gifts of Peace and Joy

Receiving the gift of love is a simple, two-step process; yet we make it complicated. The first step is to forgive, and the second is to expect love to flow naturally to you. When you forgive, you open yourself to receive love. Forgive yourself for the times you did the wrong thing, said something dumb, hurt someone's feelings, lied to yourself, lied to others, and just messed up all around. Part of your process of forgiveness may include a heartfelt apology to the person you hurt. It may be an internal conversation during which you let yourself know that you acknowledge that you have not been kind with yourself or honored the special being that you are. No matter how long or short the conversation with yourself, you must end with "for that, I forgive you."

Once you forgive yourself, you must then forgive others for the hurt that they may have intentionally or unintentionally inflicted on you. Forgiving others does not mean that you continue to open the door for them to come in and use and abuse you. Forgiving others means that you are committed to the healing process, which requires that you let the past go and make better decisions for the future.

When Jesus died on the cross, He asked God to forgive those who persecuted Him. When He rose from the dead, He didn't go back to them so they could do it all over again. I say this not to be sacrilegious but to underscore to those who are abused that forgiveness does not mean going back to be abused all over again. Love does not punch you in the face one day and kiss you the next as a routine. That is not love. That's a sickness, and if you are in such a relationship, I have two words for you: *get out!* Then follow it up by getting help!

You were not meant to be anyone's punching bag. You do not deserve to be abused if you forgave someone before. Forgiveness is for *you!* It allows you to move forward and make a clear decision about what is best for you. It clears your spirit and puts you on the path to being made whole again. It is the balm that will help heal your brokenness, disappointment, hurt, and emotional pain. You should not repeat the same pattern or the same mistake.

Remember, when Jesus forgave sinners, He typically said, "Go and sin no more." I love the passage in which He healed the crippled man at the pool of Bethesda. He said, "See, you are well again. Stop sinning or something worse may happen to you" (John 5:14). I don't know what the man had done before, but I'm sure that after he was forgiven, he heeded Jesus' last words to him. I know I would have! Forgiveness is for you. You have a do-over and can do something differently, better, and with more wisdom.

After you forgive, the second step is to expect love to be part of your life. You must welcome it back home like a long-lost friend. It will come, because love always comes when it is welcomed. It just waits for you to open the door and move out of the way.

As I write this, I am on my lanai, listening to the wind as it rushes through the trees. The sun highlights the hue of the grass and the leaves, which are a mixture of light green, jade, red, amber, and brown. The birds chirp and squawk as squirrels scamper up and down the trees, looking for food, mating, or playing. My trusted companion, my Maltese Misty, walks around, inspecting the perimeter; the latest addition to the family, a rambunctious Yorkie puppy, sits comfortably on my lap. My daughter opens the sliding door and says, "Good morning, Mommy." She then kisses me on my check to complete this circle of love.

> Love always comes when it is welcomed. It just waits for you to open the door and move out of the way.

I'm a love magnet! And, dear reader, so are you! Just expect it, welcome it, take a deep breath, and embrace it, because it is always there. It waits for you. Be ready, open, and accepting, because when it comes, it brings all the goodness that your heart can hold. It may not come how you expect it. It may come in watching leaves rustle across the grass. It may come in someone buying you a cup of coffee that day. It may come in a warm smile from someone in the grocery line. Just grab it! Catch it quickly like the gift from heaven that it is. Let it complete its purpose through you and for you. It came to heal, give, and provide overflowing joy and peace.

Basking in Love

You can spot a couple in love a mile away. Usually, they are the ones holding hands, smiling at each other. They're the ones you spot at the table across from you in a restaurant who make googly eyes at each other; he feeds her, and she takes food from his plate. They laugh and are engaged in a deep conversation, making eye contact and enjoying each other's company. When you spot them, you may just want to smack them! Or you may feel bad that you don't have that for yourself or that you once had it and now it's gone. If you can't relate (or if you don't want to admit that you can relate), that's okay.

I tried an experiment one day. I went into a local restaurant and had dinner by myself! I thought I'd feel lonely. I thought people would stare, but if they did, I didn't realize it, because I was just grateful to have a moment of peace by myself. I was also proud that I had the courage to walk into the restaurant and have lunch alone. I didn't need company or want it that particular day. I had come a long way from yearning to fit into the image of having someone to eat with and worrying about what other people thought if I didn't have someone to eat with. You may think that's lame, but I truly had an issue with not having a date until I realized that I didn't *have* to have a date to feel comfortable in a public setting with couples making googly eyes at each other! I had enough love for myself to be by myself, enjoy my company, appreciate the peace of the moment, and be grateful that I came such a long way in self-acceptance and self-love.

What I admire most about couples in love is that they bask in it. Whether they are together or apart, you can see a glow on their faces. They are usually smiling, and some seem to glide through the air as they walk. There's something different about them. That's how we all should be every day of our lives, because we are loved by a beautiful, awesome, and gracious God. If we thought about His love for just a moment, we would be like a person in love—smiling, gliding, and completely full of joy and hope.

The disciple John basked in Jesus' love, and he knew that Jesus loved him. There was no doubt in his mind that Jesus loved him even more than the other eleven disciples! He was constantly near Jesus, leaning on Him and following Him to the cross. If you read John's gospel cover-to-cover, he always referred to himself as "the one whom Jesus loved." At the Last Supper, he said, "Now there was leaning on Jesus' bosom, one of his disciples, whom Jesus loved" (John 13:23).

John must have just been content and confident in the full knowledge that Jesus loved him. There is no indication in the Bible that John ever doubted that. He received the gift of Jesus' love and loved him in return, which was apparent when he followed Him all the way to Calvary. At the foot of the cross, John 19:26 says, "When Jesus saw his mother there, and *the disciple whom he loved* standing nearby, he said to his mother, 'Dear woman, here is your son,' and to the disciple, 'here is your mother.' From that time on, this disciple took her into his home."

John is also referred to at Jesus' resurrection, when the women did not find His body at the tomb. John 20:2 says, "So she came running to Simon Peter and the other disciple, the one Jesus loved, and said, 'They have taken the Lord out of the tomb, and we don't know where they have put him.'" He is mentioned again when Jesus first revealed Himself to the disciples: "Therefore that disciple whom Jesus loved said to Peter, 'It is the Lord'" (John 21:7). John 21:20 says, "Peter, turned and saw that the disciple whom Jesus loved following them. (This was the one who had leaned back against Jesus at the supper and had said, 'Lord, who is going to betray you?')."

John must have been like those couples who are in love. He must have held his head high when he walked the streets of Galilee with Jesus, since John was the one whom He loved. He must have introduced himself as, "I'm John, the disciple Jesus loves." I wonder if he had the bumper sticker and the T-shirt. If not, I'm sure Jesus' love glowed all over his face.

That's how we should all be! We, like John, are loved by God. If you think about it every day and truly meditate on His goodness, there would be no need to wonder if we are loved! This morning, I was very grateful to see the sun rise in the sky as I drove down the highway to come to work. I thought to myself, Thank you, *Lord, that I see another sunrise. There will be a day when I won't!*

God loves me! He gives me an opportunity to breathe yet one more day! Yesterday, I almost got hit by a truck. It was my fault! I veered into the turn lane and didn't see the truck in the mirror but then got a quick glance of it before I pulled completely over. *Phew!* Thank God, He loves me! My daughter just called me at work to ask me, "Mommy, how is your day?" *Thank you, Lord. You sent me another sign that You love me.*

If we meditate on the goodness of God and the love of His Son, Jesus, how can we not walk away glowing and radiant? Just knowing that makes me want to go out and glide down the sidewalk, smiling from ear to ear. I don't know about you, dear reader, but I want to be like John. I want to know that I know that I know. I want to just rest on Jesus' bosom, knowing that I am the disciple whom Jesus loves! I want that peace in knowing that no matter what, I can rest on His bosom; I am the one He calls into His inner circle. I am loved and in love with my Creator, so I can be confidant and full of joy, basking in His goodness and mercy every day, all day! I want someone to look at me and wonder, *Is she in love?*

Giving Love: Return to Sender

When you receive the gift of love, you must give it back to yourself and to someone else. When you do this, you complete the circle of love so that more love and goodness can flow to you. Sometimes, we forget this concept. There are some who receive love and horde it; they do not give it back. There are others who receive love but do not accept it, so they can't give it back. Some of us don't receive love, because we do not know how to accept it, so we have none to give back.

Everything in life is a circle. You've heard the adage: what goes around comes around. Well, that's the same thing with love. When you are open to love and receive it, then you are obligated to give it back to someone else. It could be in the smile you give to the clerk at the drive-thru window. You were there to get a hamburger, but you gave a warm smile of appreciation. It could be allowing someone with a few groceries to go ahead of you in the shopping line. You were there to buy toiletries, but you gave a kind gesture to make someone's day. Maybe it comes in the act of stacking the dishes at the restaurant table and not leaving a mess for someone else to clean up after you. *Ouch!* Or maybe it is returning your shopping cart to the caddy and not leaving it in the parking space next to you for someone to hit when they pull into the spot.

When you do any good deed from a place of love, it comes back to you, because you return love to its source. In other words, you do something from a loving place, so only love and compassion can come back to you. You may say, "Well, that hasn't happened to me. I work at a place where people are nasty to each other and unprofessional. I don't see any love coming back to me." Just wait. It will. It may not come back from the person you give it to, but it will find you! Remember, you are a love magnet. You can't hide from the source of love or from the gift love has for you!

I dealt with an ugly issue at work. A coworker in another department sent someone I supervised a nasty, condescending e-mail and carbon-copied me on it. I responded professionally and directly, letting him know that I thought his e-mail was unprofessional and that I'd be happy to meet him to discuss his concerns. In our discussion, his face was red, and he said how offended he was that I had the nerve to call him unprofessional. Instead of proving how right I was and how wrong he was, I directed the conversation on how we could move forward from there. After that meeting, he was always guarded in how he addressed me or anyone in my department.

A few years later, I saw this man in the hall way with his daughter, whom he had picked up from school, and he asked her if she wanted to meet me, because I was a nice lady. Now, I'm not sure how genuine he was in what he told his daughter, but I was grateful that those words came from his mouth. Because I handled the prior situation from a place of gentleness and didn't let my ego take control, I set the tone for only goodness to flow. The compliment was love returning to me from what I gave years before.

In that example, the goodness of love came from the same individual back to me; however, sometimes, you do not experience the love you gave from the same person. I think that's the hardest truth to swallow. We think that when we give love to someone, we should get it back from that person. It doesn't always happen that way. Our job is to just love and let love return to us in the way in which we need to have it. Don't force it to come to you. Don't wait expectantly for it to come a certain way at a certain time. Just know that it will come, and when it does, receive it as the gift of goodness that it is.

I wish that I knew this concept years ago. It may have saved me some heartache in my relationships. I think many of us get mixed up when we expect people to be like us or give like us. Some people are not in a place to give or receive love. Don't be disappointed if they do not reciprocate love. You keep loving, giving, and expecting it to manifest itself to you in various ways.

There's a song called "Looking for Love in All the Wrong Places." I had a friend who probably should have written the lyrics to the song, because she lived them. She gave love to different men and looked for them to return it to her in the same way she gave it to them. She bought gifts for them, paid for dinner, and listened to their problems—even about their wives. That was the road she traveled—looking for love in all the wrong places.

When you love yourself and are open to love, you will give love and receive it in kind. That doesn't mean that you give love to a married man and expect him to love you the same way. That is definitely not what I'm saying! Loving yourself and being open to love will steer you on the path to getting the love that you *need,* not the love that you *desire* or *want.* When the love that you need comes into your space, you will be able to inhale it as effortlessly as you do your daily breath. When I sat on my lanai, love came to me. I needed to feel love, peace, and oneness that morning. I needed the gentle kiss from my daughter and to know the love of our pets surrounding me. I had a rough week, and what I needed, love gave back to me in those few moments. I may have wanted to have breakfast served to me by a dozen muscular men. If I concentrated on that image of love, I may have missed receiving the love that I needed.

That week, I gave love to all those around me. I didn't discriminate in who I gave my love and kindness to. Sometimes it was easy to laugh with a coworker whom I enjoyed having a conversation with, and at other times, it was difficult to say a friendly hello to a colleague who I knew was making trouble for others on the job. But love does not discriminate or differentiate between those who deserve it and those who don't. It just is.

I have often wondered why Jesus died for sinners like me. Why would He want to leave His throne of glory to come and be spat on by those lower than Him; ridiculed by hypocritical Pharisees; called a liar by the sons of Adam, who told the first lie;

rejected by His friend; and betrayed by someone who ate supper with Him? Why would He choose to give up His life, lay down on splintered wood, watch men hammer nails into His flesh, and hang mercilessly and painfully for all to see? I sure would not have wanted such a fate.

I love my daughter, and I would go through those things for her so that she would not have to. If the choice was given to me to be crucified or let her die, I would choose crucifixion so that her life would be spared. Parents put love first all of the time. Maybe it's not a dire choice, like crucifixion, but parents hurt for their children and want to wipe away their pain. It hurts any parent when his or her child is rejected.

At my daughter's first day of preschool, I wanted her to be accepted by the students in her class. I wanted the teacher to like her and see how special she was. I wanted the best for her. If I could have gone through the first day for her, I would have. I just don't think I could fit in those seats! When she went to middle school, she was not one of the popular kids. She said she sat at the cafeteria table by herself and ate lunch. My heart broke. The next day, I left work early and had lunch with her. Although I couldn't have lunch with her every day, I wanted to just so that she would not feel rejected and alone. I then sent her notes of encouragement every day until she finally found a lunch friend.

Love took on our rejection, shortcomings, hatred—in short, our sins. It did not discriminate between those we like and don't like or between those we think deserve it and those we don't. Love just did it for all so that everyone would have the same opportunity for everlasting life.

Therefore, when we love, we must not discriminate—and

that is hard! We must love the person we think deserves it and the person we think doesn't deserve it. The same people we think don't deserve it may think the same thing about us just by our actions toward them! The hardest thing to do is to be kind to someone who is unkind and gentle to someone who is a jerk.

I ran into a person whose actions are ugly, prideful, and greedy. She does underhanded things to get what she wants. In the ladies room, we dried our hands at the sink, and I wanted to just give her the silent treatment. But I asked her about her children's first day of kindergarten. Her eyes lit up, and she beamed at how the one who was adopted adjusted well; however, her other child needed more time to adjust to the new classroom. That may not mean much to you, but at least I wasn't nasty to her and shared the same conversation I would share with someone who I thought deserved my time.

When you open yourself up to the opportunity to love, you release your divine gift to receive love. It comes back to its source. The few moments of kindness I gave the woman in the ladies room left her feeling that someone cared enough to ask about her children's first day. I did not receive anything from her that day or in that moment, and I do not expect to get anything from her. However, I expect love to show up from some place and return to me what I gave. It will probably come from an unexpected source. Maybe it will come from someone who doesn't think that I deserve it. However it comes, I know it will, because I am open to giving and receiving it. In a sense, I've made room for the goodness of love to come into my life.

It's not easy to be open to love, but we are divinely capable of doing it. After all, it's our nature. We are called to be expressions of love—to have, nurture, and receive it. My sincere wish for you is that you remember that you are loved and have love all around you. Be open to it. Remember to love yourself first. Then be willing to accept love for what it is, not what you expect it to be. Finally, be courageous enough to give it away freely to everyone you come in contact with—even those who you don't think "deserve it" or are worthy of your kindness, patience, or time. That truly is a challenge.

Remember that we all have moments when something we say or do indicates that we may not deserve or be worthy of love. That's where forgiveness steps in and reminds us that we can have a do-over. Most importantly, be willing to receive love in the form it comes to fill your every need. You can start by accepting the simple gifts that life gives you by being grateful for your breath, your heartbeat, and the wind blowing on your face. When you receive love's gift, then you agree with your Creator that you are divinely made and deserving of all that is good and wonderful!

When you do this, love can show up in any way to complete you. It may show up in the form of a child you've been praying for, relief from debt, or a new car in your driveway. It may show up in a thank you from someone you least expect, a kiss on the cheek from your child, or the wet nose of a puppy trying to get your attention. Love could show up in a promotion at work, new furniture, or the person of your dreams staring into your eyes while the shadow from the palm tree innocently sways, your invited guests sigh, and you exchange a tender kiss. However love shows up, be open to it! Be receptive, willing, and accepting. It came to pour its goodness on you!

EMBRACING THE MESSAGE

Be Open to Love: Making Room for Goodness

🌿 Step into the new day of letting love pour over you, renewing you with a new outlook on what love is.

🌿 Love yourself, accept love for what it is, and be courageous enough to give it away freely.

🌿 When you open yourself up to the opportunity to love, you release your divine gift to receive love. It comes back to its source.

Scripture Reflection

For God so loved the world that he gave his one and only Son, that whoever believes in him shall not perish but have eternal life.

—John 3:16

Journal Notes: Be Open to Love

Before answering the questions below, have a meeting with yourself. Let yourself know that you acknowledge that you have not honored the special being that you are. Think about the times when you have criticized yourself, said hurtful things about yourself, or called yourself unkind names. Now take your imaginary eraser, and erase it all. It's done. It's over. Now say to yourself, "For all of those things, I forgive you." You're ready to begin the exercise below.

1. How do you accept the love that is around you?

2. What is the difference between the love that you need and the love that you want and desire?

3. How did love show up in your life today? List at least five signs and examples of love that you experienced.

4. What do you hide from yourself that prevents you from freely welcoming love into your life?

5. How is resting a form of receiving love? Do you struggle with this concept? If so, why?

6. How can you show yourself how much you appreciate the love around you?

7. What was the most defining message from this chapter?

8. How will you implement it in your life?

Remember, forgiveness is for *you!* It allows you to move forward and make a clear decision about what is best for you. It clears your spirit and puts you on the path to being made whole again.

CHAPTER 8

Enjoy the Gift of Peace

Then he got in the boat, his disciples with him. The next thing they knew, they were in a severe storm. Waves were crashing into the boat—and he was sound asleep! They roused him, pleading, "Master, save us! We're going down!" Jesus reprimanded them. "Why are you such cowards, such faint-hearts?" Then he stood up and told the wind to be silent, the sea to quiet down: "Silence!" The sea became smooth as glass.

—Matthew 8:23–26 (MSG)

Every time I read the Bible story of Jesus calming the storming sea, I am amazed. I am awestruck by the fact that He got up, told the wind and sea to shut up, and they did! I am floored that He asked the disciples why they were afraid, because I would have been, too. It's only natural. I am inspired that Jesus remained at peace through it all! He slept during the storm. When He acknowledged it, He sent it away! Wow!

There have been many storms in my life. Some have been

short-lived, and some have stayed a long while. There are even daily ones that I deal with on a constant basis. You know the ones—your child gets a low grade on a test, your family member needs money, or you're not feeling well. The storms come. Some sit and hover, while others pass as quickly as they arrive. However, what I know for sure is peace, faith, and courage will overcome them all.

The lesson I take away from the story of Jesus calming the sea is that no matter what, Jesus has my back, and all I need to do is stay in peace. But how do you do that? How do you not lose your everlasting mind when stress piles up, you get bad news, you don't feel like being bothered, and you don't want to be your divine self? I have had plenty of days when I've told myself, "Okay, no matter what, you are going to remain calm and peaceful." In my heart, I am more peaceful than Mother Teresa herself. But then an issue comes out of nowhere that steals my joy and robs my gift of peace.

The issue could be the coworker who says a dumb thing at the wrong time. My instinct is to slap him physically, but instead, I do it verbally. Peace is lost. It's the supervisor who once again hands me a last-minute project that he sat on for the past few months and is now due. Naturally, I'd like to tell him off and then hand in my resignation, but instead, I tell several friends, hoping they'll say something to make me feel better. Peace is stolen. Or it's my child, who can't get the simple math problem that I've explained to her for the last hour while complaining that her teacher should have taught the lesson correctly in the first place. I'm irritated; my daughter is frustrated, and we both go to bed worked up and upset. Peace is destroyed.

Life's challenges can rock us like a boat in the roaring sea. But we have to remember that we can choose to panic, like the disciples did, or we can choose to listen to the inner voice (your divine self) telling us, like Jesus told the waves, to be at peace in the midst of the storm. I choose peace. I choose to reconnect with the gift I was given a long time ago while I moved around in the fluid of my mother's womb in comfort and at peace in my own space.

Reconnecting with Your Peace

Imagine being surrounded by the soft sound of water moving back and forth. You're warm and relaxed, without a care in the world. You're safe and fearless, surrounded by all that you need. You're in a state of peace and serenity, where you move with the ebb and flow. You stretch and grow, but inside your bubble of peace.

We can get back to that state of peaceful bliss as long as we reconnect to our natural inclination to be calm and connected to all that is good. Today (a typical day for me), I had what felt like fifty million e-mails in my inbox, a blinking light on my phone indicating messages to return, back-to-back meetings with employees and supervisors, homework to review when I got home, tests to help my daughter study for the next day, phone calls from my mother, lunch to pack, dinner to prepare, etc. But on this day, I wasn't at all stressed. In the midst of it all, I locked into my peace. I was peacefully connected!

How did I do this? First, I promised myself that I was going to be peaceful, no matter what came my way. Truthfully, I made my mind up to be at peace. Then I promised myself that I would do something that day that I enjoyed that would promote my peaceful state. During my lunch, I went to the local library, and there I reconnected with my peace. I plugged back into the place where I could hear my own voice and relaxed my mind. I enjoyed browsing through the DVD titles, wondering which one I would choose for my weekend lounge on the couch. I loved reading my magazine as I sat in the backyard patio of the library. I took my shoes off, sank in the cushioned chair, embraced the quiet, and deeply breathed in the moment of solitude.

I was in the zone, or "experiencing moments of presence," as Eckhart Tolle calls it in *The Power of Now*. Then when I got back to the job, I could finish out my hectic day and go home to my task-driven evening. I had, in essence, told the wind in my life to shut up, because I chose peace. My day continued to be hectic, but the chaos was on the outside and not on the inside of me. Peace was restored.

Besides enjoying the twenty minutes I had in the library, what I truly enjoyed most was that I was more in control of myself, which made a difference in how I handled my day. I called my friend that evening, told her how my day went, and suggested she try to do what I did the next day. She followed these steps and called me the next evening to tell me she thought that she had more time in her day and had the opportunity to sit down and work on some personal projects (something she had been trying to do for the last year).

You may say, "Melissa, I wish I could find a peaceful moment in my day. I don't work close to a library where I can go for lunch. And even if I did, the library does not have a backyard patio."

Please don't miss the point. You may not be near a library with a backyard patio, but as long as you connect to the quiet and peace within yourself, you will find a way. Here are some other suggestions: take a walk, go to a local coffee house for lunch (sometimes they serve sandwiches), sit in your car with your most peaceful and favorite song playing, go visit a local church, or go to the local park. The point is to promise yourself to stay in peace, make an effort to take your mind off of the situation, and reconnect to your natural peaceful state. It's where your divine self radiates, longing for your recognition and return.

Make a Commitment to Peace

No matter how upset, angry, and frustrated you may feel, that is not your natural state. No animal is naturally upset, angry, or frustrated. By and large, unless the animal is threatened or looking for food, it is calm and peacefully goes about its daily routine. As I write this, my Maltese is lying down by my foot while a lawnmower buzzes in the background. And guess what! The birds that chirped in the trees this morning while I drank my coffee still chirp through the noise that threatens to steal my peace. Nature is perfectly peaceful, and so are we. However, I think we forget to stay in harmony with that peace even though we can reconnect and tap into it at any time.

> Make a peace pact with yourself. Make a commitment to stay at peace, no matter what happens in your day.

Make a peace pact with yourself. Make a commitment to stay at peace, no matter what happens in your day. There is power in making up your mind to stay in harmony with yourself. You put the world on notice that you will only react in one state, and you will not allow the nonsense to steal your joy.

Scripture tells us to set our minds on things above, not on earthly things (Colossians 3:2). Abraham must have known this. When his servants were in conflict with his nephew, Lot's, servants over the land between Bethel and Ai, Abraham told Lot to look over the land and take whatever he wanted so that they could keep the peace (Genesis 13:8–11). Lot took the best part of the land (the Jordan valley) and left Abraham with little to nothing in Canaan. Still, God blessed Abraham, and his land prospered. As promised, he became the father of many nations.

Joseph knew about the power of peace when he was thrown in jail for something he did not do (Genesis 39). He stayed in peace, didn't complain, and was promoted to the second in command to Pharaoh. Ruth picked up leftover wheat, even though she did not have a way to take care of herself and her mother-in-law, Naomi. She held her tongue, didn't complain, remained obedient, and received a blessing from Boaz (Ruth 2).

Daniel kept his peace in the lion's den (Daniel 6). Shadrach, Meshach, and Abednego kept their peace as they felt the heat from the furnace. King Nebuchadnezzar gave them one final chance to bow before the false god he had made. But they refused, saying, "If we are thrown into the blazing furnace, the God we serve is able to deliver us from Your Majesty's hand. But even if he does not, we want you to know, Your Majesty, that we will not serve your gods or worship the image of gold you have set up" (Daniel 3:17–18).

The king threw Daniel and his friends into the fire, but God saved them by sending His Spirit. King Nebuchadnezzar then said, "Weren't there three men that we tied up and threw into the fire … Look! I see four men walking around in the fire, unbound and unharmed, and the fourth looks like a son of the gods!" (Daniel 3:24–25) They all learned the lesson of making a commitment to staying at peace, and they were rewarded for it. That should make you shout for joy! Locked in jail, thrown into a lion's pit, flung into a fiery furnace, or bending down to pick up scraps of wheat, these men and women knew the power of connecting to their peace, and each was rewarded in mighty ways.

These great men and women understood the power of staying committed to peace. I, however, learned this lesson the hard way. As a director of technology, I have one of the most stressful jobs in my school district. Technology does not always work, and it is not magic. I am known for my "you've got to be kidding me" moments when I get upset about something that is so ridiculously dumb and innately wrong. The way to push my buttons is to be unfair and irrational, which people do quite frequently where I work.

A button-pushing incident happened at work, and one of the employees told me about it. He explained the issue, and before he got to the "sock it to ya" part, he prefaced it by saying to another employee standing in our circle of conversation, "Now, she's going to hit the roof when I tell her this." I concentrated so much on what he said that I missed the "sock it to ya" part. To this day, I don't even remember what was supposed to make me mad. I did not want to give him the satisfaction of seeing me lose control.

He then looked at me and asked, "Doesn't that get to you?" I calmly gave him directions on what to do about the issue and walked back to my office. I realized that in some way, I gave up my power to remain at peace when I let someone know how he or she could push my buttons. I determined from that point forward that no matter the issue, I would remain calm. I wouldn't give anyone the opportunity to predict when I was going to hit the roof, even though I am passionate about being fair and doing the right thing all the time, not when it is convenient or easy.

It gives me much pleasure when employees tell me something that would flip me out and I am able to shock them by remaining calm. How do I do it? I make my mind up every day to stay connected to my peaceful state. I'm not the Dalai Lama by any stretch of the imagination; however, I am determined not to lose my peace and enjoy every moment of my life.

You should, too! Determine not to fly off the handle about everything or some things. Make up your mind that you will stay calm, no matter what the cost. That doesn't mean that you do not express your emotions and say when something is upsetting or unfair. However, it does mean that you react to it from a powerful state of peace about how you are going to handle the situation and yourself as opposed to losing your mind, control, and in some cases, your life.

Stress can truly kill you. We can get into an academic discussion over whether stress is real or just a person's perception, but the fact still remains that constant demands on our time and effort create stressful situations. Over time, reactions to these stressful situations can lead to health-related issues. I got a call the other day from my younger brother, who has two kids, owns a home, and works a full-time job and two part-time jobs. He told me that his chest hurt, and he felt that he couldn't breathe. After going to the emergency room, the doctor told him that he was hypertensive, and the doctor would have to run more tests to ensure that his organs were properly functioning. That was a game-changer for him. Now he makes his mind up every day to not only take care of his health, but also stay at peace and enjoy it!

Inviting Peace Back into Your Space

Your supervisor is on the phone, irately asking for a report; you just got a nasty e-mail from an employee who has no idea what he is talking about but blames you for the problem; you woke up late, and now you are running around the house, trying to get ready; the dog decides to poop on the carpet; you arrive at your child's school just in time and look in your mirror to see the red and blue lights of a patrol car. How do you enjoy your peace every day, given the stressful situations that come your way? How do we enjoy peace in times of storms?

No matter what the situation, how you react to it determines whether you will maintain or lose your peace. It comes down to a simple choice. I don't know about you, but I am tired of Satan laughing at me and stealing my joy. Since he roves around the earth, looking for whom he can destroy (Job 1:7), I don't want to make his job easy. I don't want to lose any more time getting bent out of shape and letting circumstances take from me what is rightfully mine. I guess I have an attitude about keeping my peace. I have power when I look at every situation and I think about how I can keep my peace. I am not always successful and fall short, but I am determined to get up and reconnect with the peace that dwells within me.

Each of the stress-filled examples that I gave have happened to me. I wish I could say that in every circumstance, I was peaceful and took the high road, but I can't. I was far from being in a peaceful state! But I began to realize that I caused some of the storms in my life! I created some of my stressful situations by not communicating, not going to bed early, not walking the dog, etc. I'm not saying that each and every situation is your fault, but I encourage you to determine what part of the situation you could avoid if you did something differently to encourage a peaceful situation. I call this inviting peace back into my life.

Peace does not reemerge in your life unless it is accepted and embraced. Peace is always there, but you must *choose* to acknowledge it. You have to support it by doing and thinking about things differently.

In our hectic society, it takes deliberate effort to support and nurture our peaceful state. Here are a few peace-boosters that should be nonnegotiable in your life.

> Peace does not reemerge in your life unless it is accepted and embraced. Peace is always there, but you must choose to acknowledge it.

Get enough rest for obvious reasons—to help you reduce fatigue, stay focused, and maintain balance. As Ben Franklin said, "Early to bed, early to rise, makes a man happy, wealthy, and wise." As David said," In vain you rise early and stay up late, toiling for food to eat—for he grants sleep to those he loves" (Psalm 127:2). I'm very glad God gives us His beloved sleep. That is all I need to give myself permission to get to bed and stop worrying about things that I can't control the next day.

Eat well and regularly. Be sure to include energy-boosting fruits and vegetables and lots of water. Your brain is made up of 90 percent water, and needs at least eight glasses a day for normal function. The truism "an apple a day keeps the doctor away" is a good reminder. Paul stated that "So whether you eat or drink or whatever you do, do all for the glory of God" (1 Corinthians 10:31).

Plan ahead, and refuse to wait until the last minute to complete projects. Remember, haste makes waste, and God always has a plan even for us (Jeremiah 29:11). I planned so much that I was criticized for it. Planning is not only the key to success, but also the key to keeping your peace about a situation. I was comforted when I read Rudy Giuliani's book *Leadership.* He detailed how he and his staff always planned and even had contingency plans. They even practiced their contingency plans and acted out their possible scenarios. He credits all of this planning to effectively handling the September 11 crisis that shook the world.

Give yourself more time to get to your destination, get dressed, or do whatever needs to be done. Rushing increases stress and decreases peace. Haste makes waste. King Solomon said, "There is a time for everything, and a season for every activity under the heavens" (Ecclesiastes 3:1).

Think things through by allowing yourself enough time to reflect. It will help you stay true to your heart and keep you aligned with your true intentions. In William Shakespeare's *Hamlet,* the character Polonius advises his son, Laertes, "To thine own self be true." Paul reminded us, "Do not conform to the pattern of this world, but be transformed by the renewing of your mind. Then you will be able to test and approve what God's will is—his good, pleasing and perfect will" (Romans 12:2).

Simplify your schedule by prioritizing and not trying to do everything in one day. I love that the Creator of our universe had to rest on the last day and even tells us to remember the Sabbath day and keep it holy.

Begin your day with prayer by meditating on the goodness of God. When you are in a grateful state, you set your mind at ease and allow for the possibility of all that is good to flow to and through you. Every morning, I start my day with some type of prayer or reflection. Groggy, I open my devotional, read Scripture, and sometimes write in my journal. On my way to work, I listen to peaceful music, and when I go to work, I go in the bathroom, kneel, and pray, asking God to go before me and order my steps for the day. I don't do this because I am spiritual but because I *need* it. I *need* to be in tune with God in order to stay connected to my peace.

Jesus did it, and He is the Son of God! The Word says, "Very early in the morning, while it was still dark, Jesus got up, left the house and went off to a solitary place, where he prayed" (Mark 1:35). The gospel goes on to say that Simon found Him there, praying, and told Him that everyone was looking for Him. He then had a busy day laying hands on the sick. If the Son of God rose early to pray, what does that say about me? Praying early (even for a few minutes) helps to frame your day, puts your mind at ease, and keeps things in perspective.

You may have heard this advice before, but maybe hearing it again will remind you to slow down, reprioritize, reschedule, think, and then embrace your calm, natural state. Then you can rest while the waves crash, because everything within your control will remain at peace.

Inviting Peace into Your Conversations and Relationships

A very helpful neighbor went across the street and picked up some leaves from her neighbor's lawn. She left the bag of leaves by the curb, where it would be picked up the next day. The woman thanked her neighbor for such a kind gesture. However, the woman's roommate was up in arms when he found out that the neighbor had taken it upon herself to walk on *his* grass and pick up *his* leaves without permission and then leave the garbage bag on the curb. He called her all types of names, including a busybody. He then took the bag of leaves and threw it on the kind neighbor's lawn, which led to an unnecessary argument over a gentle act.

It is very important to choose peace and invite it into our conversations daily. If we do, we will alleviate the levels of strife and stress that we sometimes create foolishly. In the situation with the two neighbors, the man's intention was to make *his* presence known. Instead of seeing the kind gesture for what it was, he decided to create drama and tension. However, before we judge him, we need to look closely at ourselves and the times when we take situations and turn them into messes of hostility and aggravation.

The only thing to do to avoid this peace-stealer is to invite peace into our conversations with people. Instead of having the goal to tell someone off or put someone in his or her place, we should try to leave the conversation with understanding and cordiality toward each other. We can agree to disagree. However, we can walk away from the exchange peaceably and peacefully.

I got off the phone with a nail technician after a conversation that could have gone south fast, because I felt wronged. The night before, I treated my mother to getting her nails done. They were not done well, as the polish was lumpy. The next morning, my mother called to tell me that she had tried to put clear polish on her nails to try to make them look smoother, but when that didn't work, she just took off the polish altogether. I called the nail salon.

Before I even said a word to the technician, I told myself, *My goal is to let her know that I am not angry but that I paid for a service that I did not get.* After calmly going back and forth with her about whose fault it was for not telling her last night that the nails were torn up, I finally said, "Again, I am not angry; however, I thought it was important for you to know that I am not pleased with the service that I paid and tipped you for. I didn't want to stop coming to you without you knowing my displeasure with your service." The phone call ended with her offering to give a 50 percent discount the next time we come in and an apology. I was calm, she was calm, and I got more than I asked for. My peace was undisturbed—mission accomplished!

When you invite peace into your conversations, you can only end up winning in the long run. It works with your children, spouse, friends, and employees. Most people do not want to be angry at each other or in heated situations. If you find yourself in one, ask yourself, *What can I do to stay peaceful?* It is more important to walk away with your peace than feel the inner reward of being right. Although you may be right once and win the conversation, you may lose your power, peace, and self-control. Staying at peace even if you don't get to put the person in his or her place is always the better option. When you walk out of the room and leave the stormy situation, people will marvel at you and say, as they said about Jesus, "What manner of man is this that even the winds and the sea obey him!" Your peace will be intact! That's one black eye for Satan!

Inviting peace into your conversations sometimes means keeping your mouth closed, even when you are right. That is hard for me! I'm learning that sometimes, just not uttering a word is best when I'm in a no-win situation. If you know a person is argumentative and always has to have the last word, why continue to argue? Once you've made your point, why lose your peace over a fool? Proverbs 23:9 says, "Do not speak to fools, for they will scorn your prudent words." Proverbs 26:5 says, "Answer not a fool according to his folly, or he will be wise in his own eyes."

Sometimes, to keep your peace, you must hold your tongue. Our Savior did this when He was sent before Herod and Pilate. He was about to die, yet the Bible says He did not say a word (1 Peter 2:23). He did not open His mouth but kept His peace, knowing the mission He came to accomplish and knowing that no matter what He said, they would not believe or release Him.

Sometimes, to keep your victory and peace, it's best not to answer. It's best to hold your peace so that you can be the winner. You're not upset. You haven't given away your control. More importantly, you've taken the high ground and are a better person for it. Holding your peace could equate to keeping your job, restoring your marriage, or healing a bond between you and your child. Knowing when to keep your mouth closed is truly a gift unto itself. It's not only peaceful, but also life-giving.

Giving Our Gift of Peace Away

When we give our gift of peace, we offer others the best of ourselves. We offer them the best of who we can be. It takes commitment to reconnect to our peaceful states and stay in peace. It is even more powerful to give peace away! There are some people you love to be around, because they have peaceful and calming natures. There are others who you know if you told them some disturbing news, they would handle it calmly and without getting too upset. They exude peace and have little trouble giving their peace away freely.

Giving away peace is a daily task. I have to remind myself and consciously work on it. Although peace is our natural state, it is not in my nature to be peaceful. Some people just have a calming personality that radiates peace. I have a calm demeanor, but I can also be quick-tongued. Before I know it, words are spoken, and peace is destroyed. Sometimes, I've even taken pride in unleashing my tongue and walked away, saying, "Now they know where I stand" or "I bet they won't do that again." The sad thing is that I've said this about people I supposedly love. I know that truly loving them means giving them my peace even if I feel it's undeserved.

I'm learning to respect my gift of peace. I'm learning to reconnect to what Christ freely gave me. He teaches me that peace is acceptance. It's accepting the situation for what it is but remaining focused enough to not let the situation affect me on the inside. Peace is radical. It's the opposite of what people expect. They think I'm going to argue, but I say a calming word. Peace is obedience. It is learning to be tuned to God and follow what He tells you do, not what your flesh wants to do. Peace is humbling. It's learning to back down, even when you are right, for the sake of staying at peace. Peace is vigilant. It always looks for a way to restore order and balance to life. Peace is love. It's unconditional and unbiased. It's loving a person enough to say, "Because I love you, I'm not going to say something to hurt you." Even if you do not know a person, peace loves Jesus enough to say, "Because I love you, I'm not going to hurt you by hurting this person."

We have this peace. We have the gift that Christ left us after He rose from the dead on Easter morning. He could have left us gold, riches, or the wisdom of great kings. He could have left us eternal life. But as He ascended, He looked out on the world and said, "Peace I leave with you; my peace I give you. I do not give you as the world gives. Do not let your hearts be troubled and do not be afraid" (John 14:27). He left us the most powerful gift—His peace.

Jesus knew what we'd face. He knew that we would struggle with temptation, as He did when the Devil tried to tempt Him three times. He knew we'd struggle with backstabbing, as one of Jesus' disciples did when he sold Jesus for thirty pieces of silver. He knew we'd face false accusations, as He did with the Pharisees. He was certain that we'd be treated unfairly and encounter lies, deceit, arrogance, nepotism, jealousy, gossip, plots, schemes, etc. He knew this, because He experienced it and acknowledged it when He said He was sending us as lambs among wolves. Yet He left us His peace. His peace must be powerful, then! It must be a gift that is so wonderful that it can conquer all that He left us to face.

We just need to remember that peace dwells in each of us. We just need to remember that we have it with us always. Here's the most beautiful part—since it is a gift that we are given, then we can, in turn, give it away. Not only do we have this divine power of peace, but we can also give it to others at any time and in any situation.

We can give peace away when the baby cries and the toddler pulls at our skirts. We can hand it to our son when he asks us for the fifth time to play ball, even though we have housework to do. We can give it to the supervisor who is off the wall over a trivial spelling error. We can give it to a spouse who turns all of our white laundry blue. We can even give it to a stranger who cuts us off in traffic, takes our parking spaces, cuts in line, interrupts our conversations, or hands us back the wrong change. In our daily lives, we can give peace. If we stay connected and remember who we divinely are, we can conquer situations and not lose our cool about them.

That's what I'm hoping for and working toward. Even if I struggle to do it, I'm committed to keeping my gift of peace so that I can pass it on to others. Are you?

EMBRACING THE MESSAGE

Enjoy the Gift of Peace

❧ Reconnecting to your peace is daily refocusing on what you were born to be from the time you were in your mother's womb.

❧ A commitment to peace is a sacred contract between yourself and God. You say you're willing and ask for His help. He hears and rewards you for your commitment.

❧ No matter what the situation, how you react to it determines whether you will maintain your peace or lose it. It comes down to a simple choice.

❧ Inviting peace into our conversations sometimes means holding our tongues.

❧ When we give our gift of peace, we offer others the best of ourselves.

Scripture Reflection

You will keep in perfect peace those whose minds
are steadfast because they trust in you.

—Isaiah 26:3

Journal Notes: Enjoy Your Peace

This page is intentionally left blank for you to artistically express your ideas on peace. Cut out pictures from newspapers and magazines that demonstrate some of the principles in this chapter.

You can reflect on your selections by asking the following questions:

1. What does peace mean to me?

2. How can I reconnect to my peaceful nature?

3. How do I show my gift of peace to others?

Feel free to paste your pictures below as a reminder that you are a divine expression of peace and have the power to give it away.

Remember, peace is acceptance. Peace is radical. Peace is obedience. Peace is humbling. Peace is vigilant. Peace is love.

CHAPTER 9

Epilogue:
The True Journey Begins

The crowd of students and family members sat intently on the bleachers as the sun slowly set behind the makeshift stage on the football field. The graduates were all seated in defined rows with their square blue caps and matching satin gowns. There was electricity in the air as each speaker detailed his or her four-year journey that had come to an end.

But when the senior class coordinator took the stage, the students thundered with overwhelming applause. She recalled their time at the school and gave vivid examples of her experiences with them, from school fundraisers and football games to homecoming and senior prom. Then she told them to remember to live their best lives and give all they could as they headed on to the next chapter of their lives. She closed her moving speech by yelling out, "YOLO!" The graduates began to say, "YOLO" in response, nodding their heads in agreement and turning to each other in laughter.

I'm glad the speaker then explained to us not-so-hip folks that YOLO stands for "you only live once." When she said those words, I reminisced about my graduation, which was much like the one I was attending. I remember the details as distinctly as I now remember this graduation. Her words have stayed with me, because not only do you only live once, but you also don't get to repeat what you did years ago. I will never have a high school graduation again. I will never be able to go back in time and recreate the circumstances, take hold of the opportunities, replay my actions, or change the choices I made.

If I could, I would change all of the times that I did not believe in myself. I would erase the doubt and fear that I was not able to handle the situation, make the right choice, or give all that I had within me. I would tell that senior girl about to graduate and take on the world that she had everything necessary to move forward. She had all of the confidence, will, determination, and ability needed to be successful in life, because she is divinely made. Back when I was a teenager, time was of no consequence, and life seemed like a dress rehearsal.

The saying "you only live once" should remind us that we do not have time to wallow in despair and self-depravation. We were put here for a purpose, and that purpose is to live the lives that we are given to the fullest. Don't waste any more time going down the avenue of self-pity or wandering down the street of self-doubt. We are wonderfully and perfectly made in the image of the divine Creator of this universe. There is no reason for our heads to be bowed in any circumstance or situation.

I truly pray that after reading this book, you will get that message! I hope that you will see that no one can take from you what you already have. No one can take your power from you. No one can take away your beauty. It was divinely given to you from the source of all goodness and mercy, so don't give it away! Don't cower in a circumstance, because you are supremely made. Don't drown in self-pity, because you have the blood of biblical kings and queens running through your veins. Don't forfeit your potential, because Jesus died so that you could live life to the fullest. Fight to keep the gifts that He gave you, from the love He showed when He dropped His head and died to the peace He left when He went back to the perfection from which He came.

The saying "you only live once" should remind us all that living is a precious gift of which we are deemed worthy. I love what Bob Gass says: "When you stumble or face a problem, God doesn't jump off His throne and say, 'John is in trouble, Mary's in a mess, I'd better act!' No, He's *already* placed all that's necessary to handle the situation and overcome it."[7]

God is not surprised by anything that happens in your life. He's not surprised when the supervisor overlooks you for the promotion, a loved one hurts your feelings, or you lose your temper with your children. God gave you and me all that we need to overcome our circumstances, defeat the odds, and be more than conquerors! He gave us all of the resources to succeed and be triumphant in this life!

I am overjoyed that God has that much faith in me! I am very glad that when He sent us on this journey of life, He packed our

---

7   Bob Gass, *The Best of the Word for Today, Volume II* (Denver, CO: Synergy Publishers, 2003).

bags with everything that we need. He sent us with more than enough love, power, beauty, abundance, and peace to survive on this trip. It is up to us to reach into our bags and remember what we have and who we are. We are spectacular! We are extraordinary! We are divinely enough!

I pray that we never forget who we are. I pray that we always tap into our true selves when we are at our lowest and that we always remember that we have the tools to overcome obstacles, confidently meet challenges, and live the abundant lives we were called to live. If we can do that, then our daughters will reap the benefits of our examples. They will also remember their divine calling: to be daughters of the Most High God, uninhibited, unshakeable, and unashamed!

As I leave you to continue on your travels, I send you all of the love that your heart can hold. Be at peace, my friend. Hold your head high, and walk boldly every day of your life. You came with a purpose and have all you need to accomplish it, no matter what life throws your way. You are a divine creation in every way. Put your shoulders back, and hold your head high, for you are divinely made. I pray that you will always remember that and that it will forever change your life!

Be blessed,
Melissa

My Dearest Katieri,

You were born in love. You are the reflection of love. I love everything about you, from your thick, long black hair to your red, polished toes. You were born perfect in our sight. We doted over you and adored you just because you were a gift of love to us. Never forget that. Don't let anyone tell you differently. There is nothing wrong with you. You have everything that you need. Remember to always love yourself. Love yourself for the gift that you are, and know that you are here specifically to offer your gifts. You are love. You are loved. Love sent you here to me. Nothing can separate or change the love I have for you—not space, not time. It will be with you in your heart even when I am no more. I love you always, so always love yourself!

With all my heart,
Mommy

ABOUT THE AUTHOR

Melissa Harts is the proud mother of beautiful thirteen-year-old Katieri. She credits her faith in God and belief in Jesus Christ for helping her through life's challenges. She remains humbled by the grace and gifts God has given her, including her educational experience. She is the coauthor of the book *Schools that Make the Grade: What Successful Schools Do to Improve Student Achievement.* Melissa is a native New Yorker who now resides in Florida.

41052207R00115

Made in the USA
Lexington, KY
27 April 2015